CRIMES OF HONOUR

Formal and Informal Adjudicatory Systems in India and Pakistan To Enforce and Contest Honour Crimes

MOHAMMED SUBHAN HUSSAIN

SULIS ACADEMIC PRESS

An Imprint of Sulis International Press
Los Angeles | Dallas | London

CRIMES OF HONOUR: FORMAL AND INFORMAL ADJUDICATORY SYSTEMS IN INDIA AND PAKISTAN TO ENFORCE AND CONTEST HONOUR CRIMES

ISBN (Print): 978-1-958139-00-4
ISBN (eBook): 978-1-958139-01-1

Published by Sulis Academic Press
an Imprint of Sulis International
Los Angeles | Dallas | London

www.sulisinternational.com

Contents

This study is dedicated to my late father Sajjad Hussain for his encouragement of my interest in pursuing postgraduate research. I wish to acknowledge the help of Professor Werner Menski (Emeritus now). His work instilled in me the spirit of questioning, and acknowledgement is due for that. I would also like to thank my supervisors Meghan Campbell and Natasa Mavronicola at the University of Birmingham, for their feedback and support.

INTRODUCTION

> *'All are equal before the law and are entitled without any discrimination to equal protection of the law. All are entitled to equal protection against any discrimination in violation of this Declaration and against any incitement to such discrimination'.*[1]

International human rights instruments such as the Universal Declaration of Human Rights (UDHR), the International Covenant on Civil and Political Rights (ICCPR),[2] the International Covenant on Economic, Social and Cultural Rights (ICESCR),[3] and the United Nations Convention on the Elimination of All Forms of Discrimination against Women (CEDAW)[4] embody some of the most fundamental human rights and ensure equal protection under the law. However, even decades after the adoption of the UDHR and other human rights instruments, several customary practices violating the dignity of human beings and their fundamental rights continue to persist. One such practice is that of honour crimes.

---

[1]Universal Declaration of Human Rights 1948, art 7.

[2]International Covenant on Civil and Political Rights 1966, arts 3 and 26.

[3]International Covenant on Economic, Social and Cultural Rights, arts 2(2) and 3.

[4]Convention on the Elimination of All Forms of Discrimination against Women, arts 2(c), 2(g) and 5(a).

Although they occur in many parts of the world, this study focuses on honour crimes in India and Pakistan, which share a common historical context that is also reflected in their cultures, legal systems, and social dynamics. Both countries have communal societies where the group or community exerts a strong influence on individual members.[5] The rights of the individual are subordinate to those of the community, and individual members of society must abide by the laws of the community. In both societies, the reputation or honour of a person or community is the most important factor in identification and prestige. Honour plays an important role in an individual's relationship with their community and has a great influence on important life decisions.[6] Any act or behaviour that negatively affects the honour of the family or community can have negative consequences for the individual, including honour crimes. 'Honour crimes' generally refer to different types of crimes committed mainly against women to protect the so-called 'honour' of the family. The term is commonly used as shorthand, to flag a type of violence against women characterised by (claimed) 'motivation' rather than by perpetrator or form of manifestation.[7] 'Shame killings' or 'honour killings' occur because the perpetrators believe that the victim has brought shame, disrespect, and/or dishonour to their family or has violated the community and/or religious rules and principles. Human Rights Watch (HRW) defines an honour crime as '*an act of violence, usually murder, committed by male family members*

---

[5] Lindsay Hughes, 'India-Pakistan Relations – Part Three: Economic and Cultural Aspects' (2016) Future Directions International <www.futuredirections.org.au/publication/india-pakistan-relations-part-three-economic-cultural-aspects/> accessed 26 July 2021.

[6] Patricia M Rodriguez, 'The Role of Honour Concerns in Emotional Reaction to Offences' (2002) 16 Cognition and Emotion 143.

[7] Lynn Welchman and Sara Hossain, Honour: Crimes, Paradigms, and Violence Against Women (1st edn, Zed Books Ltd 2005) 7.

against female family members who are perceived to have brought dishonour upon the family'.[8] These crimes are committed to protect the honour of the family. Women who are accused of dishonouring their families and societies by engaging in what is considered disrespectful are subjected to different types of violence. However, there are no fixed criteria to determine the moral value of an act. Activities that are considered inappropriate and disrespectful are judged subjectively. The standard for appropriate behaviour varies according to religion, social class, cultural background, and region. Extramarital affairs, marriages outside one's community, love marriages, clothing that is considered provocative in the respective culture, etc., are generally considered inappropriate.

As most honour-based violence disproportionately targets women,[9] it is often considered a gendered crime. This is reflected in UNICEF's definition of honour crimes as 'an ancient practice in which men kill female relatives in the name of family 'honour' for forced or suspected sexual activity outside marriage, even when they are the victims of rape'.[10] The HRW and UNICEF definitions focus on the acts of violence committed against women.[11] The definitions suggest that they are committed to protect and/or defend the 'honour' of a family or com-

---

[8]Human Rights Watch, 'Integration of the Human Rights of Women and the Gender Perspective: Violence against Women and "Honour" Crimes' (2001) Intervention Before the 57th Session of the U.N. Commission on Human Rights.

[9]ibid.

[10]National Commission for Human Rights, 'A Study on Honour Killings in Pakistan and Recommendatory Checks through Law' (2019) The Office of the Chairman, National Commission for Human Rights, Government of Pakistan <https://nchr.gov.pk/wp-content/uploads/2019/01/Final-Report-Honour-Killing.pdf> accessed 26 July 2021.

[11]P Chesler and N Bloom, 'Hindu vs. Muslim Honor Killings' (2012) 19 Middle East Quarterly 43.

munity.[12],[13] General Recommendation No 31 of the Committee on the Elimination of All Forms of Discriminations against Women[14] declared honour crimes as a form of violence that is rooted in gender roles assigned based on the customary practices of different cultures. Men are assigned the task of controlling women's sexual behaviour, whereas women are expected to adhere to a culturally defined set of behaviours. By adhering to these norms, women protect the honour of the family. If a woman violates social norms, she is accused of bringing shame to her family and society. In patriarchal societies, women are considered the guardians of their families' honour. Therefore, men commit honour crimes against women who have violated cultural norms in order to reinforce cultural practices, protect the family's honour, and force women to strictly follow them through severe punishments.[15]

This study treats all forms of crimes committed not only to protect the reputation and honour of the family or community, but also to avenge the shame or dishonour caused by a person's involvement in inappropriate activities, as honour crimes. Although most honour crimes are committed against women to control their sexuality, they can also be committed for other

---

[12]Office of the High Commissioner for Human Rights (OHCHR), '15 Years of the United Nations Special Rapporteur on Violence Against Women, Its Causes and Consequences' <www.ohchr.org/Documents/Issues/Women/15yearreviewofVAWMandate.pdf> accessed 26 July 2021.

[13]Zara Ismail, 'The Communal Violence Bill: Women's Bodies as Repositories of Communal Honour' (2020) 21 *Journal of International Women's Studies* 50.

[14]UNGA, 'Report of the Committee on the Elimination of All Forms of Discrimination against Women General Recommendations'.

[15]Tanya D'Lima, Jennifer L Solotaroff, and Rohini Prabha Pande, 'For the Sake of Family and Tradition: Honour Killings in India and Pakistan' (2020) 5 Indian Journal of Women and Social Change 22.

reasons and against men.[16] Honour crimes are committed against male and female victims who have breached the respect and honour of the family, society, or community.[17] This study focuses on the honour crimes directed not only against women, but also against men because of their relationships with women in India and Pakistan, and assesses the factors that contribute to honour crimes in these countries. It seeks to define the role of formal and informal legal systems in both countries in addressing honour crimes. The focus is on accountability mechanisms that can provide redress and challenge underlying norms. The analysis can help us determine which system is more effective in eliminating honour crimes, suggest measures that should be taken to address this persistent problem, and expand our understanding of the deeply-rooted cultural practices based on discrimination against women and the communal groups that foster these habits.

The study is divided into four chapters, which deal with understanding the problem of honour crimes, the factors that contribute to these crimes, as well as the analysis of formal and informal justice systems and the gaps in these systems. The study proposes three-tier criteria as an analytical framework to compare, contrast, and determine the efficacy of the formal and informal adjudicatory systems, in the process of addressing honour crimes. The criteria for the effectiveness of both systems: (i) the ability of the adjudicatory mechanism to recognise transgressions; (ii) the compatibility of judgments with principles of gender equality; and (iii) whether such judgments can offer tools to redress or remedy honour crimes. The term 'gender equality' refers to the standards of equality among women,

---

[16]Pratiksha Baxi, Shirin M Rai, and Shaheen Sardar Ali, 'Legacies of Common Law: "Crimes of Honour" in India and Pakistan' (2006) 27 Third World Quarterly 1239.

[17]ibid.

men, girls, and boys, which prioritise non-discrimination on the basis of gender and seek to ensure that both genders are able to access and enjoy their civil, political, economic, social, and cultural rights.[18] For contextual purposes, and to broaden the legal parameters in which honour crimes are expounded upon, provincial, appellate, and higher court judgments are analysed in this study.

The first chapter describes the common historical context of India and Pakistan, which goes back thousands of years and has witnessed the rise and fall of several civilisations. Different rulers have influenced the indigenous cultures and social structures of both countries. The study of their shared history is essential to understand the evolution of formal and informal legal systems in both countries. I believe that honour crimes originated in the patriarchal systems introduced by foreign invasions and were not originally part of the indigenous culture of the subcontinent.

The second chapter focuses on the formal and informal systems of justice in India, with an emphasis on the development of law after Partition. The legal instruments enacted by the legislative bodies have adapted to the changing needs of society. The Parliament has enacted and amended penal laws to prevent honour crimes, whereas the judiciary plays a crucial role in the adjudication of such cases. This chapter looks at the legal instruments enacted by the Indian Parliament and the precedents set by the courts against honour killings. It analyses some of the key precedents set by the courts and examines their role in the development of the law. It also discusses India's informal justice system, namely the Khap Panchayat, and its role in enforcing cultural norms and enabling the commission of honour

---

[18] 'OSAGI Gender Mainstreaming - Concepts and Definitions' <https://www.un.org/womenwatch/osagi/conceptsandefinitions.htm> accessed 22 August 2021.

crimes. The chapter describes how the Khap Panchayat exploits social support to ensure compliance with cultural norms. It imposes penalties and sanctions on those who violate cultural practices and contribute to violence and crime in the name of preserving community honour.[19] The chapter assesses the challenges in the formal and informal systems in order to identify the one that is most effective in dealing with honour crimes. The analytical framework will be applied to examine the socio-legal shift influenced by patriarchal norms, which created a paradigm wherein recognition, compatibility, and redress became esoteric reveries, in addressing honour crimes.

The third chapter focuses on the formal and informal adjudicatory systems in Pakistan. After Partition, Pakistan adopted the penal laws enacted by the British. However, over time, these penal laws were amended. Although the British laws provided for the defence of grave and sudden provocation in honour crimes, the amendment to the penal laws and the incorporation of *Hudood*[20] laws repealed the defence of grave and sudden provocation and incorporated the Islamic provisions of *diyat*[21] and *qisas*.[22] The Qisas and Diyat Ordinance provided impunity to the perpetrators of honour crimes. Thus, the laws in question remained subject to severe criticism. The Legislative Assembly enacted specific legal provisions to address hon-

[19]ibid.

[20]Hudood is an Arabic term that refers to Islamic penal law or Quranic punishments. In traditional Islamic legal systems, hudud is implemented when certain proofs and conditions are met. Hudud offences as stipulated in the Quran include theft, brigandage, adultery, and apostasy.

[21]In Islamic Law, Diyat refers to the financial compensation paid to a victim or their legal heirs in the case of murder or bodily harm or property damage.

[22]In Islamic Law, Qisas refers to the right of the heirs of a murder victim to demand the execution of the murderer.

our crimes and amended the Qisas and Diyat Ordinance. The chapter describes relevant judicial precedents in Pakistan and the flaws in the formal adjudicatory system. It also discusses the informal adjudication system, including the Panchayat and Jirga.[23] These institutions work in parallel with the formal adjudicatory system and ensure strict compliance with tribal and cultural values by imposing sanctions and penalties on those who violate established norms, and thus contribute to the prevalence of honour crimes. In comparing the formal and informal adjudicatory systems in Pakistan, the third chapter assesses the propinquity between formal and informal judgments, and their compatibility with principles of gender equality, pursuant to providing condign redress to victims.

The fourth chapter compares the formal and informal judicial systems of India and Pakistan, focusing on the evolution of laws in both countries after Partition. It also looks at the similarities and differences in the judiciary's approach to honour crimes and analyses the sentences passed by the higher courts in both countries. It also examines the informal institutions of the Panchayat and Jirga and the factors that have consolidated them in both countries. The analysis of legislative instruments, judicial precedents, diktats issued by the Khap Panchayat, and the role of the Jirga in addressing honour crimes shows that the formal judicial system plays an important role in protecting human rights in India and Pakistan. By applying the analytical framework, this study shows that while the legislations and judicial precedents have protected the victims of honour crimes by imposing serious penalties, the informal adjudicatory systems have promoted honour crimes. These institutions have perpetuated honour crimes and other forms of violence to ensure strict compliance with inhuman cultural norms and prac-

---

[23]ibid.

tices. In doing so, they have not recognised the grave wrongs that have been committed, and thus their adjudication remains incompatible with the principles of gender equality that intend to provide redress. With public support, these informal institutions enforce their judgments. Therefore, informal institutions should be regulated by legislative bodies and their activities prescribed by national law.

I conclude by saying that the formal system, comprising laws enacted by legislative assemblies and the judicial system, is more effective in recognising honour crimes, promoting the principles of gender equality, and providing redress and remedies to victims. The Khap Panchayat and Jirga have used violent means, including honour crimes, to consolidate their positions.[24] These institutions should be regulated and made accountable to the formal system. I propose recommendations to fill the gaps in the formal judicial systems of both countries. Measures should be taken to ensure that the judiciary is more effective, fit for purpose, and accessible to all. I also offer recommendations to amend certain provisions of the law in both countries to ensure greater legal protection.

[24] Anamika Singh, 'Honour Crime and Khap Involvement: Threat to Human Rights' (2014) 24 Deliberative Research 28.

CHAPTER 1
FORMAL AND INFORMAL ADJUDICATORY SYSTEMS IN THE SUBCONTINENT

After Partition in 1947, India and Pakistan developed their legal systems.[1] However, the impact of their shared history is reflected both in their social, political, economic, and cultural ethos, and in their culture of honour crimes and the development of formal and informal legal systems to deal with them.[2] To better understand the formal and informal legal systems of both countries, it is essential to consider their common historical context. This chapter looks at the history of honour crimes in the subcontinent, the factors that contributed to it, the development of legal instruments under colonial rule, and the informal legal systems that prevailed in the subcontinent before Partition. Understanding the common historical context is essential to understand the evolution of laws in both countries and can help us appreciate and interpret the precedents of the courts in honour crimes cases. It is also crucial to examine the origins of the Khap Panchayat and Jirga, which operate in parallel with

---

[1] Shantanu Chakrabarti, 'Interpreting the Legacy of Partition in the Sub-Continent: Indian and Pakistani Perspectives' (2016) 40 Politeja 21.

[2] Chesler (n 11).

the formal judiciary in both countries, as well as the social support mechanisms for enforcing the judgments of these informal institutions and the social structures behind them.

The Transition from Matriarchal to Patriarchal Societies

The history of the subcontinent goes back thousands of years. Its diverse religious practices, social values, cultural norms, and customs reflect the imprint of various civilisations.[327] About 4500 to 5000 years ago, the Indus Valley Civilisation, one of the oldest and most influential civilisations of the subcontinent, flourished here. Sir John Marshall, an Englishman who discovered the remains of the Indus Valley Civilisation at Mohenjo-daro, one of the oldest sites in the world, believed that women occupied a special place in society and that the Indus Valley Civilisation was a matriarchal society that worshipped goddesses. He theorised:

> *In no country in the world has the worship of the Divine Mother been so deep-rooted and ubiquitous as India. Her shrines are found in every town and hamlet throughout. She is the ... prototype of power ... which developed into that of Sakti. Her representatives are the ... village goddesses ... who one and all are personifications of the same power ... That like the Mother Goddesses of Western Asia they originated in a ma-*

[327] Ishwar Modi, 'Society and Sociology in India: Some Reflections' (2012) 178 Polish Sociological Review 141.

> *triarchal state of society is a highly reasonable supposition.*[4]

This statement shows that women played an important role in the religious sphere during the Indus Valley Civilisation. Sir John Marshall pointed out that 'the female elements appear to be co-equal to, if not predominant over the male elements'.[5] However, the position of women in public life is contestable, because there are no significant remains of the civilisation to determine their situation.

The arrival of subsequent civilisations changed the dynamics in the subcontinent. Aryans, Scythians, and Mughal Muslims introduced different practices that influenced the Adivasi indigenous[6] communities in the subcontinent. The Aryans influenced the indigenous culture and religion and introduced male-dominated practices, which affected the existing matriarchal norms negatively.[7] They consolidated the caste system to maintain their racial supremacy, banned inter-caste marriages, introduced polygamy, took women as slaves, and banned polyandry.[8] With the arrival of the Scythians and the rulers of Mughal Muslims, the status of women deteriorated further. The custom of purdah, namely veiling, excluded women from pub-

---

[4] Hannah Fane, 'The Female Element in Indian Culture' (1975) 34 Asian Folklore Studies 51.

[5] John Marshall, *Mohenjo-Daro and the Indus Valley Civilization* (2nd edn, Probsthain 1931).

[6] 'Adivasis' is a collective term used to refer to several indigenous communities in India. Adivasis are officially known as 'Scheduled Tribes'.

[7] Sarla R. Murgai, *Women in South and South East Asia* (1st edn, University of Tennessee 2004).

[8] Naresh Rout, 'Role of Women in Ancient India' (2016) Odisha Review 42.

lic life and confined them to their homes.[9] Muslim women lived within the confines of the house and covered their bodies completely when they went out. Under Mughal rule (1526–1857), Muslim women who practised purdah were respected in society.[10] Therefore, upper-caste women adopted this practise and confined themselves to their homes. The spread of veiling among Muslim and upper-caste women influenced the lower caste women, as well. These practices led to the separation of public and private life, with women withdrawing into a private sphere and their influence on public life diminishing. This way, the societies in the subcontinent gradually changed from matriarchy to patriarchy.[11] This transition resulted in the deterioration of the position of women in society. However, it sheds light on male dominance in rural parts of Northern India, which have reported the highest number of honour crimes. As a result of the dense Muslim population, rural areas and parts of Northern India, became accustomed to adopting Muslim cultural norms without formal adjudication or oversight.[12] This led to a rural/urban divide that enabled the rural feudal system to control adjudicatory processes.[13] The influence of foreign invasion

---

[9]Karin A Deutsch, *Muslim Women in Colonial North India Circa 1920-1947: Politics, Law and Community Identity* (1st edn, Cambridge 1998).

[10]Tanvir Anjum, 'The Emergence of Muslim Rule in India: Some Historical Disconnects and Missing Links' (2007) 46 Islamic Studies 217.

[11]Sharad Patil, 'Some Aspects of Matriarchy in Ancient India: Clan Mother to Tribal Mothers' (1973) 2 Social Scientist 42.

[12]J Auboyer, *Daily Life in Ancient India: From 200 BC to 700 AD* (Phoenix Press 2002).

[13]J Briggs (trs), The Rise of the Mahomedan Power in India: Power in India Till the Year A. D. 1612' (Originally written by Muhammad Kasim Ferishta, Tarikh-i Firishta, Vol. II, Arthur Probsthain 1829).

contributed to the consolidation of patriarchal norms and escalated different forms of violence against women.

Among Hindus, the caste system caused the deterioration of the status of women, particularly of the upper caste.[14] As rulers influence people of upper castes, the upper-caste women emulated the practices of Muslim women to improve their social standing.[15] The customs of 'sati', which refers to the burning of a widow on her husband's funeral pyre as an act of devotion; 'purdah', which refers to the act of covering the face and other parts of the body; and seclusion, which refers to the separation of women from public life and their confinement within their homes, were practised mainly by upper-caste women.[16] They also had to abide by other strict restrictions. Their right to freely choose a spouse was severely restricted, and they were only allowed to marry men from their own or a higher caste.[17] These restrictions were imposed to protect the superiority of the upper caste and preserve their purity. In comparison, foreign invasions – especially Muslim rule – had a smaller impact on lower caste women, who worked to support their families despite financial problems.[18] These women were discriminated against because of their caste and in many cases, were not allowed to participate in activities with upper-caste women.

---

[14]Nidhi Shrivastava, *The Progress of Indian Women from 1900s to Present* (1st edn, University of Connecticut 2009).

[15]N Hussain 'Women as objects and women as subjects within fundamentalist discourse' in N S Khan, R Saigol, and A S Zia, (eds), *Locating the Self: Perspectives on Women and Multiple Identities* (ASR Publications 1994).

[16]Bal Ram Nanda, *Indian Women: From Purdah to Modernity* (1st edn, Advent Books Division 1990).

[17]Paul D LeBlanc, 'Indus Epigraphic Perspectives: Exploring Past Decipherment Attempts & Possible New Approaches' (Master's thesis, University of Ottawa 2013).

[18]ibid.

However, the invasion of foreign rulers had a smaller impact on them than on the upper-caste women who had to bear the burden of these foreign rules. Lower caste women, for example, were entitled to many freedoms and were not bound by sati and purdah.[19] Similarly, the remarriage of widows was common among the lower castes, who continued to worship the Mother Goddess and other female idols.[20]

Honour Crimes in the Subcontinent

Foreign invasions and rule in the subcontinent had a great impact on the role of women in society. The cultural practices introduced by the invaders led to a shift from matriarchal to patriarchal societies.[21] An important aspect of a patriarchal society is the notion of family honour.[22] Honour is a social construct that determines the parameters to maintain the honour of a family.[23] The communal values of the subcontinent attributed great importance to honour and protected it by all means.[24] As Zara Ismail noted,[25] the rights of the family and community were considered more important than those of an individual;

---

[19]Mazhar-ul-Haq Khan, *Purda and Polygamy: A Study in the Social Pathology of the Muslim Society* (Nashiran-e-Ilm-o-Taraqiyat 1972).

[20]ibid.

[21]Carol P Christ, 'A New Definition of Patriarchy: Control of Women's Sexuality, Private Property, and War' (2016) 24 Feminist Theology 214.

[22]ibid.

[23]Jim Doris, 'A Conversation with Margaret Visser: Diagnosing That Feeling of Helplessness' *Catholic New Times* (Toronto, 1 May 2003).

[24]Kaushambi Kaushal, 'No Honour in Honour Killing: Comparative Analysis of Indian Traditional Social Structure vis-à-vis Gender Violence' (2020) 5 ANTYAJAA: Indian Journal of Women and Social Change 52.

[25]Ismail (n 13).

therefore, the rights of the individual were not taken into account and all possible means were used to protect the honour of the family. The patriarchal nature of the subcontinent linked honour with women's sexuality. Therefore, women and their sexual behaviour were seen as guardians of the family honour.[26]

Kamla Bhasin and Ritu Menon explained that 'most men and women agreed that honour, for losing and preserving, is located in the bodies of women'.[27] Society had established standard practices to control women's sexuality and placed the responsibility on men to ensure that their female family members adhered to these practices. A violation of standard practices by women was considered a breach of the social code, and the women responsible for inappropriate behaviour were accused of bringing shame to the family.[28] Therefore, male members of the family exercised control over women's sexuality and ensured the observance of customary practices that both protected family honour and conveyed masculine virility. If the men did not fulfil their responsibility and control, it would significantly undermine their masculinity.[29]

The standard practices of morality set by society to regulate women's sexuality were not codified or embodied in written form.[30] They were unwritten rules interpreted and enforced by the locals. The main responsibility for enforcing the practises lay with the male members of each family. However, the fe-

---

[26]ibid.

[27]Kamla Bhasin and Ritu Menon, *Borders & Boundaries: Women in India's Partition* (1st edn, Kali 1998).

[28]Kaushal (n 47).

[29]ibid.

[30]For a pertinent analysis of such a codification in the contemporary Indian context, see Ismail (n 13).

male members and community also played a role.[31] If a woman performed an act contrary to customary practices, the reputation of both the family and community was considered at risk. These social forces thus exerted pressure to ensure compliance, which led to the commission of honour crimes. The killing of an accused woman was sanctioned by society and considered an act of great courage. As Fateh stated:

> *If a woman refused to comply with the rules set down by her cultural community, her immoral behaviour contaminated the whole family. If other strategies to make the women comply failed, the only remedy was for her male relatives to kill her in order to protect the family's honour. Such murders were culturally sanctioned and designed to uphold a specific moral order.*[32]

Social and community institutions prescribed a set of standard practices to dictate women's behaviour. Standard practices to control women's sexuality varied according to caste, religion, and locality.[33] However, certain practices were common in many areas and were introduced to control women's sexuality. These included arranged marriages, endogamous marriages within one's caste and/or religion, and modest dressing. Although arranged marriages were the social norm, it was considered a crime for a couple to marry without the consent of their family, regardless of whether both partners belonged to the

[31]V M Moghadam, 'Patriarchy and the politics of gender in modernising societies: Iran, Pakistan and Afghanistan' (1992) International Sociology 35.

[32]Navratan Singh Fateh, *Honour Killing* (1st edn, University of Toronto 2012).

[33]Surinder S Jodhka and Ghanshyam Shah, 'Comparative Contexts of Discrimination: Caste and Untouchability in South Asia' (2010) 45 Economic and Political Weekly 99.

same village, religion, or caste. Similarly, the practises of endogamy and exogamy, which refer to marriages within and outside a clan, tribe, or community were widespread. Exogamous marriages in an area where endogamy was practised were considered a crime. Similarly, endogamous marriages in an area where exogamy was practised were condemned, as the ethnographic accounts of Karen Leonard show.[34],[35]59 Society justified endogamy and exogamy. Proponents of the latter claimed that members of the same clan, tribe, or community shared fraternal relationships and were therefore considered siblings and their marriage was forbidden. Proponents of the former justified marriage within a clan to maintain tribal purity.[36]

Society in general and its male members in particular, were responsible for ensuring compliance with customary moral practices and exercised control over women's sexuality by force. The violation of cultural practices was considered a threat to the morals and honour of the family and community. Therefore, various means were used to ensure strict compliance, such as isolation, beatings, various types of torture, physical and verbal abuse, harassment, humiliation, forced marriage, restriction of movement and, in extreme cases, murder. Although most honour crimes were committed by male family members against female ones, in cases where the woman's family did not want to take action against her, society forced the family to do so by imposing economic sanctions, social

---

[34]Karen Leonard and Susan Weller, 'Declining Subcaste Endogamy in India: The Hyderabad Kayasths, 1900-75' (1980) 7 American Ethnologist 504.

[35]59 Manoranjan Mohanty. *Class, Caste, Gender* (1st edn, Sage Publications 2004).

[36]Pravesh Aggarwal 'Social Alteration in the Institution of Marriage in India' [2014] Academike <www.lawctopus.com/academike/social-alteration-in-the-institution-of-marriage-in-india/#> accessed 26 July 2021.

boycotts, and other means, thus putting unbearable economic and social pressure on the family to commit honour crimes against its female members.[37],[38]62 Although most honour killings targeted women, in many cases men also fell victim to these crimes. If a woman from a higher caste married a man from a lower caste, both partners were killed. The social attitude towards the perpetrators of honour crimes encouraged more people in the countryside to commit them.[39] This was the result of conformity to the feudal values of caste, which focus on isolation from urban society.[40] Honour killings were considered private affairs and, as there was no state mechanism to punish the perpetrators, they were not reported to the official authorities.[41]

British Influence on the Status of Women in the Subcontinent

British colonial rule influenced the laws and customs of the subcontinent positively and negatively.[42] The general policy of

---

[37]Singh (n 24).

[38]62 Abdul Hadi, 'Patriarchy and Gender Based Violence in Pakistan' (2017) 10 European Journal of Social Sciences 297.

[39]S Noor, 'Karo Kari: a curse and a crime' in S Wistro (ed), *Karo Kari. Karachi* (Weer Publication 2000).

[40]Nadia Agha, 'Kinship in rural Pakistan: Consanguineous marriages and their implications for women' (2016) 54 Women's Studies International Forum 1.

[41]Garima Singh, 'Honour-Related Violence against Women in India: Problems, Perspectives and Challenges' (2016) 5 Journal of Social Work and Development Issues 80.

[42]John Dowson, *The History of India, As Told by Its Own Historians: The Muhammadan Period*, vol 1 (Edited from the Posthumous Papers of the late Sir H M Elliot, Trubner Paternoster Row 1867).

the British was not to interfere in the personal laws of the various religious communities in order to consolidate their political power in India. They introduced many legal instruments to improve the legal status of women in the subcontinent by enacting laws to protect their rights and eliminate inhuman treatment. These instruments included the Bengal Sati Regulation 1829, enacted by Lord William Bentinck, the erstwhile Governor-General of India.[43] The regulation criminalised the practice of sati[44] and prescribed penal consequences for perpetrators and instigators of the crime. This provision influenced the social acceptance of brutal practices against women. The Hindu Widows' Remarriage Act 1856 was also a progressive legislative instrument introduced by the British in support of women's rights. It provided legal protection for the remarriage of widows,[45] which had been hitherto prohibited in society. The British enacted the Female Infanticide Prevention Act 1870[46] to eliminate female infanticide. The Age of Consent Act[47] raised the age of consent for sexual intercourse to 10 years in 1860 and 12 years in 1891. The British introduced these changes to legitimise their rule in the subcontinent.[48] They claimed that the inhabitants of the subcontinent were uncivilised and that

---

[43]The Bengal Sati Regulation 1829.

[44]The practice of burning widows alive at the funeral pyres of their husbands.

[45]The Hindu Widows' Remarriage Act 1856.

[46]The Female Infanticide Prevention Act 1870.

[47]The Age of Consent Act 1891.

[48]George C Rankin, 'The Personal Law in British India' (1941) 89 Journal of the Royal Society of Arts 426.

they had come to civilise them.[49] However, these reforms failed to effect substantial change.[50]

Some of the policies formulated by the British had negative consequences for women.[51] Before their arrival, lower caste women enjoyed freedoms such as widow remarriage and were not bound by the strict rules governing upper-caste women. However, the policies of the British affected the status of lower caste women. The British wanted uniform legislation. The laws of the Hindus in British India[52] varied from caste to caste and were not codified in a written document. Only the law of the Brahmins was codified. To ensure uniformity and equal application of the law,[53] Warren Hastings, Governor of Bengal, passed a decree in 1772 and declared the codified law of the Brahmins as the sole legal authority for all Hindus. This decision had serious repercussions for lower caste women.[54],[55] The strict rules that applied to Brahmin women, such as the prohibition of divorce and remarriage were extended to lower caste women. The decision of the Governor of Bengal denied lower caste women the right to own property and to remarry, among other things.[56]

---

[49]Varsha Chitnis, 'The Legacy of Colonialism and Women Rights in India' (2007) 64 Washington Lee Law Review 1315.

[50]Dowson (n 63).

[51]Joanna Liddle and Rama Joshi, 'Gender and Imperialism in British India' (1985) 5 South Asia Research 147.

[52]'British India' refers to the rule by the British Crown of nearly all of the Indian subcontinent, including modern day Pakistan.

[53]ibid.

[54]Rankin (n 69).

[55]ibid.

[56]ibid.

The British maintained the personal laws of the different communities of India.[57] Personal laws refer to standard practices inspired by the sacred scriptures of a particular religion. These laws govern marriage, child custody, inheritance, marital rights, property, and other civil matters. They applied only to the followers of a particular religion. For example, Mohammedan law applied only to Muslims and Hindu law applied only to Hindus.[58] Each religious community had its own personal law, with provisions based on discrimination against women.[59] For example, Mohammedan law allowed a husband to take four wives but punished women for bigamy. Provisions governing inheritance, custody of children and testimony, and numerous other provisions discriminated against women. Hindu law contained discriminatory provisions against women, too. For example, a married woman was not entitled to adopt a child, had no right to inherit property, etc.[60]

The British upheld the personal laws, with one of the prominent lawyers of the Second Law Commission of India stating, 'In the present state of the population of India it is necessary to allow certain great classes of persons to have special laws recognised and enforced by our courts of justice concerning certain kinds of transactions among themselves'.[61] The British maintained personal laws and ensured their strict application.[62] Before British rule, the religious leaders of individual communities interpreted their personal laws in line with the changing

---

[57]ibid.

[58]ibid.

[59]Liddle and Joshi (n 72).

[60]ibid.

[61]Second Law Commission for India, Report 13 December 1885.

[62]Liddle and Joshi (n 72).

needs of the society.[63] However, the British used Western-trained judges to apply the personal laws of the various communities, which had been translated from Arabic and Sanskrit into Persian and English. The translations helped the judges understand the personal laws and judge cases according to the doctrine of ratio decidendi[64] and the strict application of the precedents of previous judgments, which led to the strict application of personal laws and the reinforcement of cultural practices, including the concept of honour.

The laws enacted by the British had negative consequences for the victims of honour crimes. The Indian Penal Code (IPC), 1860 provided for criminal consequences for offences committed within Indian jurisdiction. Section 300 of the IPC states, 'Except in the case hereinafter excepted, culpable homicide is murder, if the act by which the death is caused is done with the intention of causing death'.[65] It also provides that culpable homicide committed with intent (mens rea) to cause death amounts to murder. The punishment for murder under the IPC is death or imprisonment for life. Most honour killings are committed with the intention to cause death.[66] Therefore, the penalty prescribed under the IPC should apply to perpetrators. However, Section 300 does not apply to honour killings, unlike the provision of grave and sudden provocation, which allows the perpetrators of honour killings to avoid severe sentences. Exception 1 to Section 300 of the IPC 1860 reads: 'Culpable homicide is not murder if the offender, while deprived of the

---

[63] T Naqvi and K M Korai, 'Yakta-e-Rozgar', in S Wistro (ed), *Karo-kari* (Weer Publication 2000).

[64] Rankin (n 69).

[65] Indian Penal Code (IPC) 1860, s 300.

[66] Gulafroz Jan and Khazi Munir, 'Honour Killings: A Socio-Legal Analysis with Special Reference to District Srinagar of J&K' (2018) 2 Sociology International Journal 335.

power of self-control by grave and sudden provocation, causes the death of the person who gave the provocation or causes the death of any other person by mistake and accident'.[67] This applies to cases where there is an actus reus and a homicide has been committed but the mens rea is absent. Exception 1 provides that culpable homicide committed as a result of grave and sudden provocation, accidentally or by accident, do not constitute murder because they lack the intention to commit the crime.[68] Therefore, the death penalty and life imprisonment provided by the IPC for murderers do not apply to the cases covered by Exception 1.

The provision for grave and sudden provocation is often invoked in honour crimes cases to avoid the penalties imposed in murder cases. The defence of grave and sudden provocation states that the circumstances of the case were such that the offender lost self-control and committed the offence at the height of passion, with no intention of causing death. The culture of the subcontinent, augmented with skewed gender disparities, has placed the responsibility on men to control the sexual behaviour of women. It is believed that a man's failure to control a woman's sexuality hurts the male ego, undermines masculinity, and ruins the family's reputation in society. Therefore, male family members lose self-control and commit honour killings, and invoke the defence provided in Exception 1 that the crime was committed at the height of passion, with no intention of causing the death of the victim.[69]

The judges appointed by the British to try crimes in India interpreted the provision of grave and sudden provocation and in some cases accepted the defence of the perpetrators of hon-

---

[67]Indian Penal Code (IPC) 1860, s 300, Exception 1.

[68]ibid.

[69]Jan and Munir (n 87).

our killings. Compounded with cultural norms, judicial attitudes, in a mutually exclusive manner, reinforced regressive paternalistic taboos. In *Emperor v Dinbandhu Ooriya*,[70] the Calcutta High Court held that 'It is well established that if a husband discovers his wife in the act of adultery and thereupon kills her, he is guilty of manslaughter only and not of murder'.[71] In this case, the court accepted the accused's defence. The judgment recognised that the defence of grave and sudden provocation is applicable in cases where men witness adultery, extramarital affairs, and/or similar acts by the female members of their families.[72] The judgment of the court has since been exploited by the perpetrators of honour killings to mitigate their sentences and justify their crimes in defence of so-called honour.

To successfully invoke the defence provided in Exception 1 of Section 300 of the IPC and claim grave and sudden provocation, the accused must prove that the crime was committed in the heat of the moment. In honour killings, however, perpetrators do not act exclusively in the heat of the moment. They conspire and commit the crime with a premeditated intention,[73] and later invoke the provision of grave and sudden provocation to exploit the due process of law.[74] Courts of law have accepted the defence of perpetrators in different cases of honour killings. In *Saleh Muhammad v The State*,[75] the accused was charged

[70]*Emperor v Dinbandhu Ooriya* AIR 1930 Cal 199.

[71]ibid.

[72]ibid.

[73]Mohanty (n 59).

[74]Maliha Zia Lari, 'A Pilot Study on: Honour Killings in Pakistan and Compliance of Law' (2011) Aurat Publication and Information Service Foundation <www.af.org.pk/pub_files/1366345831.pdf> accessed 26 July 2021.

[75]*Saleh Muhammad v The State* PLD 1965 SC 366.

under Section 300. He woke up late at night and was unable to find his sister in her bed. He took a hatchet and started looking for his sister and found her in a compromising situation with a man in the fields. He killed his sister and the man on the spot. Chief Justice Cornelius held that:

> *The taking of a hatchet can be explained by the fact that it was still dark, that is, for selfprotection, and it may be the accused expected to have to chastise his sister for misbehaviour if that was found. But upon the admissible evidence, in this case, there is no ground for thinking that the appellant expected to find his sister in an act of intimacy with a stranger. He must be allowed, on the evidence, the benefit of a shock, on making the discovery, such as is fully recognised in law as furnishing grave and sudden provocation within the meaning of exception I to Section 300, P. P. C., Sufficient to cause loss of self-control.*[76]

A judgment of the Supreme Court of Pakistan recognised the defence of grave and sudden provocation and all the lower courts of the country followed suit. In recognising this defence, the Supreme Court of Pakistan emphasised that the accused was in 'shock' when he found his sister in a compromising situation. The plea of grave and sudden provocation has also been recognised by Indian courts. In *K.M. Nanavati v. State of Maharashtra*,[77] the accused invoked the defence of grave and sudden provocation after murdering his wife, who had confessed to being in an illicit relationship with another man. Although the court accepted the defence of aggravated and sudden

[76]ibid.

[77]*K.M. Nanavati v the State of Maharashtra* AIR 1962 SC 605.

provocation, it found that the test for it was objective.[78] To determine whether the defence is applicable, the court must consider the reaction of a reasonable person in the circumstances, and not the particular circumstances of the accused. If a reasonable person would lose self-control in such circumstances, only then could the defendant's claim be accepted.[79] In comparison to the judgment in *Saleh Muhammad v The State*,[80] the court, in *Nanavati*, found that the accused did not commit the murder in the heat of passion, as he had allowed himself plenty of time in which a reasonable person in similar circumstances would have calmed down and it was unlikely that he would have committed the offence. The accused's sentence was therefore not reduced.[81] The cases of *Saleh Muhammad v. State* and *K.M. Nanavati v. State of Maharashtra* reflect the influence of British laws on the legal systems of India and Pakistan. While the British introduced Exception 1 in Section 300 of the IPC, the legislative assemblies of India and Pakistan have, over time, amended many provisions of the IPC in their jurisdictions.

Informal Adjudicatory Systems in Pre-Partition India: Khap Panchayat

Historians believe that the Khap Panchayat came into existence with the settlement of people in villages. In each village, there was a majority of a particular clan or caste that dictated the

[78]ibid.

[79]ibid.

[80]*Saleh* (n 96).

[81]ibid.

rules for the village.[82] Initially, the Khap Panchayat was established to ensure the security of the village.[83] Over time, however, it became responsible for ensuring compliance with customs and norms,[84] such as standard principles of morality and social practices like marriage. As patriarchal institutions, their decisions often overlook the interests and well-being of women and enforce the societal concept that links family honour to women's bodies.[85] The Khap Panchayat, mainly comprising men, employs various means to ensure strict adherence to Khap rules and traditions, making them patriarchal institutions. Anyone who violates the precepts and norms of the Khap Panchayat faces serious consequences.[86] It ensures the enforcement of its commandments and the observance of its rules through social boycotts, the imposition of heavy fines, and in some cases, the use of physical force and the imposition of the death penalty.[87] The power of the Khap Panchayat lies in the social acceptance and support for the institution.[88] Its diktats enjoy societal sanctions and are enforced by the members of society without the assistance of any law enforcement agency.

---

[82]Ayush Verma, 'Khap Panchayat: Informal Justice vs Formal Justice' (*iPleaders*, 14 September 2020) <https://blog.ipleaders.in/khap-panchayat-informal-justice-vs-formal-justice/> accessed 26 July 2021.

[83]Chesler (n 11).

[84]Suraj Bhan Bharadwaj, 'Myth and Reality of the Khap Panchayats: A Historical Analysis of the Panchayat and Khap Panchayat' (2012) 28 Studies in History 43.

[85]ibid.

[86]ibid.

[87]ibid.

[88]Shereen Sadiq and Asif Khan, 'Khap Panchayats in India: Precepts and Practices' (2015) 7 International Journal of Current Research 11753.

Informal Adjudicatory Systems in Pre-Partition India: Jirga

The Jirga is similar to the Khap Panchayat and is mainly associated with the tribal areas of Khyber Pakhtunkhwa and the Baloch tribes of Balochistan.[89] In this system, the elders of the village or tribe form the Jirga (council) and regulate local affairs. Religious leaders were also part of the Jirga when it came to religious issues. The history of the Jirga goes back hundreds of years, with some historians claiming that the system originated with Aryan tribes.[90] The Jirga was responsible for settling disputes peacefully among different tribes in particular areas[91] and by laying down rules and practices to be observed by all residents. These rules governed marriage, the custody of children and other social matters, and included a code of conduct for women. Like the Khap Panchayat, the Jirga was a patriarchal institution mainly comprising men. The decisions of the Jirga were often disadvantageous to women.[92] The Jirga places the honour of the family and community and imposes strict rules on women.[93] Women are punished if they violate the usual norms of behaviour, through physical and verbal abuse, harassment, torture, and in some cases, even death. These institutions are the main informal justice mechanisms in India and Pakistan that serve to perpetuate male-dominated practices and promote honour crimes. Although they helped encourage male members of society to commit honour crimes, the British took

[89]Chesler (n 11).

[90]Amna Mahmood, Shaukat Ullah, and Shughla Ashfaq, 'The Evolution of Jirga System: A Conflict Resolution Mechanism in FATA' (2018) 2 Liberal Arts and Social Sciences International Journal 21.

[91]ibid.

[92]Chesler (n 11).

[93]Mahmood and others (n 111).

no significant action against them. After Partition, both countries retained these institutions, which are still part of their social fabric today and contribute to the persistence of honour crimes.

Formal and informal adjudication has shifted away from benign descriptions of legal pluralism to consider how pluralistic legal systems may be viewed as fields of overlapping and intersecting subordination by victims of honour crimes. With all their complexities, diversity, and contradictions, formal and informal adjudicatory systems bring to the fore conflicting concepts of governance: at the domestic and communal levels. As a result, it is the abdication of legal intervention against non-state adjudicatory bodies that has been met with serious criticism.

CHAPTER 2
FORMAL AND INFORMAL HONOUR CRIMES ADJUDICATORY SYSTEMS IN INDIA

Honour Crimes as a National Issue

The National Crime Records Bureau of India issued a report on crime statistics for 2018,[1] which revealed that 30 honour killings were reported in the states of Jharkhand, Himachal Pradesh, Maharashtra, Punjab, Assam, Gujarat, Jammu and Kashmir, Kerala, Odisha, Rajasthan, Telangana, and Delhi that year.[2] However, the number of honour crimes and killings is even higher because they are often reported as suicides, accidents, or incidents of domestic violence. According to a report by The Hindu,[3] a daily newspaper in India, 40 percent of the 2013 rape cases adjudicated by New Delhi's District Courts

---

[1]NCRB (National Crime Records Bureau), 'Crime in India – 2018' (2019) National Crime Report Bureau Ministry of Home Affairs <https://ncrb.gov.in/en/crime-india-2018#> accessed 26 July 2021.

[2]ibid.

[3]Rukmini S, 'The Many Shades of Rape Cases in Delhi' *The Hindu* (New Delhi, 29 July 2014) <www.thehindu.com/data/the-many-shades-of-rape-cases-in-delhi/article6261042.ece> accessed 26 July 2021.

involved couples who had married without the approval of their parents. In such cases, the parents, mainly of the woman, reported false cases of rape.[4] The report indicates that honour crimes are disguised by other offences and that the actual number of honour crimes is underreported in India.[5]

Honour killings and other forms of honour crimes are not confined to a particular area or caste. They are prevalent in all parts of India, committed by members of different castes, religions, and faiths.[6] However, many individuals associate the phenomenon with particular localities. Nirupama, a journalism student, was killed by her parents in the name of family honour in 2010. She was a Brahmin, which is an upper caste, and wanted to marry her classmate, Priyabhanshu, who belonged to a lower caste. In this case, the then chairperson of India's National Commission of Women, Girija Vyas said, 'Nirupama's case could not be termed an honour killing. Khap Panchayat and honour killings are specific to Haryana'.[7] However, this statement contradicts the facts.[8] The statement also reflects the lack of acceptance of honour crimes as a national issue that cannot be restricted to a particular place. Suggesting that honour crimes are limited to a particular place overlooks the severity of the issue at the national level. Therefore, it is vital to

---

[4]ibid.

[5]ibid.

[6]Hemant Yadav, 'Honour Killings-An In-Depth study' (2012) Shamsher Bahadur Saxena College of Law <https://papers.ssrn.com/sol3/papers.cfm?abstract_id=2034965> accessed 26 July 2021.

[7]Kavita Krishnan, 'Nirupama's Murder: The Violence of the High-Born' (*Counter Currents*, 26 May 2010) <www.countercurrents.org/krishnan260510.htm> accessed 26 July 2021.

[8]OHCHR (n 12).

recognise that honour crimes are not limited to a particular area or state in India but are reported nationwide.[9]

Although most honour crimes are reported in Northern India (Punjab, Haryana, Uttar Pradesh, etc.),[10] they are also prevalent in other parts of the country. An Assistant Professor at the Department of Law at Maharshi Dayanand University, Haryana, contended that '*although most honour crimes reportedly take place in Punjab, Haryana, Delhi, Western Uttar Pradesh and other parts of Northern and Western India, other areas of India also register such incidents*'.[11] Similarly, numerous national and international organisations have reported honour crimes in southern India. They also take place in rural and urban areas, although the rate is higher in the former.[12]

Honour killings are an attempt to forcefully control the sexuality of women; they are an attack on the autonomy of women.[13] In most cases, women are the victims and are subjected to violence. However, in many cases, violence is also directed against the partners of the women. Therefore, honour crimes target not only women but also men who break the cultural diktats and the standard norms of society. For, example Nitish Katara[14] was killed in the name of honour by the sons of

[9]'Honour Killings: More than 300 Cases in the Last Three Years' *Times of India* (22 September 2018) <https://timesofindia.indiatimes.com/india/honour-killings-more-than-300-cases-in-last-three-years/articleshow/65908947.cms> accessed 26 July 2021.

[10]Bharadwaj (n 105).

[11]Kavita Dhull, 'Honour Killing in India' (2017) 2 International Journal of Advanced Educational Research 417.

[12]Nalla Ram, 'Vishakapatnam: Honour Killings on the Rise' *Deccan Chronicle* (Vishakapatnam: 18 September 2018) <www.deccanchronicle.com/nation/crime/180918/visakhapatnam-honour-killings-on-the-rise.html> accessed 26 July 2021>.

[13]Ismail (n 13).

[14]*State v Vikas Yadav & Vishal Yadav*, SC No. 78/2002.

a politician, D.P. Yadav because he was allegedly in love with their sister. In this case, the mother of the victim, Neelam Katara, recalled the remarks of the honourable judge of the Sessions Court,[15] who asked her: 'How is this an honour crime? Daughters are killed in honour crimes, but here your son was killed'.[16] This statement indicates that most honour crimes in India are associated with women victims, with the judiciary reflecting the general beliefs prevailing in society. Honour killings are a national phenomenon and are committed against either gender. This chapter analyses the formal and informal adjudicatory systems in India to identify both the role of legislation and the judiciary in addressing honour crimes and the problems in the formal system that have been contributing towards social support for the Jirga and Panchayat systems. An analytical framework is used to compare, contrast, and determine the efficacy of the formal and informal adjudicatory systems, pursuant to addressing honour crimes. The criteria for the effectiveness of either system are: (i) the adjudicatory mechanism's ability to recognise transgressions; (ii) the compatibility of judgments with principles of gender equality; and (iii) whether such judgments can offer tools to redress or remedy the crimes. The term gender-equality principle refers to the standards of equality among women, men, girls, and boys of non-discrimination on the basis of gender, and to ensure that both genders are able to access and enjoy their civil, political, economic, social and cultural rights.[17]

---

[15]ibid.

[16]Kavita Krishnan, 'Honour Crimes in India: An Assault on Women's Autonomy' (*Al Jazeera*, 2018) <www.aljazeera.com/opinions/2018/3/14/honour-crimes-in-india-an-assault-on-womens-autonomy> accessed 26 July 2021.

[17]'OSAGI Gender Mainstreaming - Concepts and Definitions' (n 18).

The Informal Adjudicatory System of Honour Crimes in India

The Khap Panchayat is an informal adjudicatory system[18] for honour crimes in India, which contributes to honour killings and other honour crimes.[19] It is different from the institution of Panchayati Raj,[20] and understanding the differences between the two is essential to understand the informal adjudicatory system for honour crimes in India. The Panchayati Raj is a local self-governance institution, whose members are elected by the people it serves. It is protected by the Constitution of India and oversees the administration of localities.[21] This chapter examines whether, in line with the analytical framework, the formal adjudicatory system inexorably supports the informal adjudication of honour crimes.

The Panchayati Raj

The institution of Panchayati Raj has been in existence in rural India for hundreds of years. It has played a significant role in the administration of justice at the village level, resolution of disputes among the inhabitants of particular villages or areas, and the social development of villages while influencing the political process of the state.[22] Article 40 of the Constitution of India recognises the importance of Panchayati Raj and directs the states to establish Panchayat systems at the village and dis-

---

[18]Bharadwaj (n 105).

[19]Singh (n 24).

[20]George Matthew, *Status of Panchayati Raj in the States and Union Territories of India, 2000* (Concept Publishing Company 2000).

[21]ibid.

[22]ibid.

trict levels.[23] Article 40 is a Directive Principle of State policy and does not impose a legal obligation on states to establish a Panchayat system. It is the discretionary power of the states to consolidate the institution of Panchayat within its jurisdiction, as a result of which some states consolidated the Panchayati Raj, whereas others did not take any steps in this regard.[24]

The 73rd amendment to the Constitution of India changed the legal status of the Panchayat system and provided constitutional protection to the Panchayati Raj. Article 243 B of the Constitution of India states thus: 'Constitution of Panchayats. (1) There shall be constituted in every State, Panchayats at the village, intermediate and district levels in accordance with the provisions of this Part'.[25] Following an amendment, Article 243B imposed a legal obligation on all states to establish the Panchayati Raj within their jurisdictions. The constitution also provides a mechanism whereby the members of the Panchayat are elected by the *Gram Sabha* (gathering of village adults). The powers of the Panchayat are listed in the Eleventh Schedule of the Constitution of India. The Constitution provides that at least one-third of the total membership of the Panchayat shall comprise women, and reserves seats for the scheduled castes.[26] The Panchayati Raj is an effective form of local government and ensures the effective administration of affairs at the grassroots level.[27]

---

[23]Constitution of India, art 40.

[24]Matthew (n 134).

[25]Constitution of India, art 243B.

[26]Constitution of India, Eleventh Schedule.

[27]Matthew (n 134).

The Khap Panchayat System

The Khap Panchayat is a community organisation that generally represents the same *gotra* (clan), caste, or village. It comprises the elders and powerful individuals of the village. These people are not elected to the position, but are self-proclaimed defenders and custodians of the norms and traditions of their village.[28] There are two levels of the Khap Panchayat. The first is the village level Khap Panchayat, where the elders and powerful members of adjacent villages participate and pronounce their judgments on various matters.[29] The second is the Sarv-Khap Panchayat, which refers to the assembly of multiple Khap Panchayats. The Khap Panchayat at the village level and the Sarv-Khap Panchayat enjoy and exercise similar powers and pronounce judgments called diktats in matters related to inter-caste, intra-caste, inter-village, and same *gotra* marriages, inheritance, property, etc.[30] Generally, the Khap Panchayat at the village level pronounces a judgment after adjudicating upon the matter under consideration. If it is serious and involves members of multiple Khaps, then the Sarv-Khap will adjudicate.[31]

The caste and *gotra* systems have developed specific norms to regulate the behaviour of and social interactions among their members. They attach great importance to these social norms and practices, compliance with which is highly regarded. These

---

[28]RE Dobash and RP Dobash, *Rethinking Violence against Women* (Sage Publications 1998).

[29]ibid.

[30]Vineet Singh, 'Khap Panchayats: Honor Killings in India' (2015) <www.researchgate.net/publication/297346507_Khap_Panchayats_Honor_Killings_in_India> accessed 26 July 2021.

[31]ibid.

norms and practices include the prohibition on marriage within the same *gotra*, village, or adjoining villages.[32] Similarly, the Khap Panchayat restricts relations among members of one caste with those of another. The norms and practices of the Khap Panchayat system impose restrictions on women's sexuality.[33] The Khap Panchayat system dates back hundreds of years, with some historians tracing its origins to the Rig Vedic times.[34] A Khap Panchayat is a community organisation with no legal standing. It is not affiliated to the Panchayati Raj institutions established by the state that operate as local government bodies. Although Khap Panchayats are present in all parts of India, they are mainly dominant in Northern India, specifically in Haryana, Punjab, and Rajasthan.[35] The Khap Panchayat wields great influence over the lives of people in enforcing norms and traditions. It ensures the enforcement of its decisions by imposing economic sanctions, social boycotts, and several other penalties on individuals who have acted against its rules.[36] Some practices and norms enforced by the Khap Panchayat are contradictory to the legislative instruments enacted by the Parliament of India.[37]

Role of Khap Panchayats in Honour Crimes

Society has developed norms and traditions to regulate the behaviour of its members. These norms and traditions impose re-

---

[32]ibid.

[33]Bharadwaj (n 105).

[34]ibid.

[35]Singh (n 144).

[36]ibid.

[37]For example, the Khap Panchayat prohibits inter-caste marriage and marriage within the same *gotra*, which is contrary to the Hindu Marriage Act 1955 and the Special Marriage Act 1954.

strictions on women's sexuality and on the freedom of choice of individuals in selecting their life partners. Anyone who contravenes the norms and traditions of society is accused of bringing dishonour to their family and community.[38] The members of the Khap Panchayat consider themselves the custodians of social norms and customs. To ensure strict compliance with its norms, they impose sanctions and other penalties on those who deviate from the expected behaviour. There are numerous cases in which the verdict of the Khap Panchayat has culminated in the commission of honour crimes.[39]

The Khap Panchayat enjoys social and political power. Families succumb to these pressures and commit crimes against their members who are accused of bringing dishonour to the family and community by violating the norms and customs of society. In some cases, the Khap Panchayats have pronounced the death penalty for couples who married within the same *gotra* or outside the same caste, and committed other similar violations. In the Manoj-Babli Honour Killing Case,[40] the verdict of the Khap Panchayat instigated Babli's family members, which resulted in the killing of the couple.158 Similarly, in numerous other cases, the Khap Panchayat has compelled young boys and girls to take their own lives, and have pressured family members or members of the community to commit honour crimes.[41]

---

[38]DK Srivastava, 'Personal Laws and Religious Freedom' (1976) 18 Journal of the Indian Law Institute 551.

[39]Singh (n 24).

[40]*Smt. Chandrapati v State of Haryana and Others* (27 May, 2011). 158 ibid.

[41]Yadav (n 120).

Higher courts in India have recognised the role of the Khap Panchayats in honour crime cases. In *Arumugam Servai v State of Tamil Nadu,*[42] the court opined:

> *We have in recent years heard of 'Khap Panchayats' (known as 'Katta Panchayats' in Tamil Nadu) which often decree or encourage honour killings or other atrocities in an institutionalized way on boys and girls of different castes and religion, who wish to get married or have been married, or interfere with (2011) 6 SCC 405 the personal lives of people. We are of the opinion that this is wholly illegal and has to be ruthlessly stamped out.*[43]

In this case, the court condemned the role of Khap Panchayats in honour killings by upholding the right of individuals to exercise their right to marry. The judgment declared the interference of the Khap Panchayat in the exercise of the right to marry contrary to the laws of India. This courageous judgment serves to support the principles of gender equality, and thus enable women to have a stronger voice in choosing their life partners. Higher courts in India have declared the existence of Khap Panchayats, pursuant to their roles in honour crimes, a violation of the Constitution of India and other instruments enacted by the legislature. Justice Markandey Katju and Gyan Sudha Mishra stated:

> *This is wholly illegal and has to be ruthlessly stamped out. There is nothing honourable in an honour killing or other atrocities and, in fact, it is nothing but barbaric and shameful murder. Other atrocities in respect*

---

[42] *Arumugam Servai v State of Tamil Nadu* [2011].

[43] ibid.

> *of the personal lives of the people committed by feudal-minded persons deserve harsh punishments. Only this way can we stamp out such acts of barbarism and feudal mentality. Moreover, these acts take the law into their own hands, and amount to kangaroo courts which are wholly illegal.*[44]

In this historic judgment, the Supreme Court declared honour crimes to be grave violations of human rights[45] and prescribed harsh punishments for perpetrators.[46] The court declared Khap Panchayats illegal, and called them kangaroo courts[47] and instructed law enforcement agencies to not only take substantial measures against the members of the Khap Panchayat but also eliminate the institution itself.[48] Similarly, in the Manoj-Babli Honour Killing Case,[49] the trial court declared the Khap Panchayat contrary to the constitution and imposed the death sentence on its leader for inciting the family to commit honour killings.[50] These judgments make it clear that the higher courts of India have established the fact that Khap Panchayats do not provide recognition to honour crimes or redress to victims.[51] Imposing harsh punishments will not only recognise the crimes committed by the perpetrators, but also allow the redress and remedy of offences.[52] The courts of law have an effective

[44] *Lata Singh v. State of U.P. and Another* [2006].

[45] ibid, para 60.

[46] ibid.

[47] ibid.

[48] ibid.

[49] *Chandrapati* (n 154).

[50] ibid, para 88.

[51] Amit Kumar Singh, 'Paradox between Universalism of Human Rights and Relativism of Culture: A Case Study of Honour Killings in India' (2020) 4 Journal of Southeast Asian Human Rights 253.

[52] ibid 267.

modus operandi to determine the infringement of the rights of people guaranteed by the legislative instruments of the state.[53] As in this case, the court declared the institution of Khap Panchayat unconstitutional and illegal based on its transgression of the law.[54] These institutions deprive people of their fundamental rights and pronounce verdicts without giving them any opportunity to be heard.[55]

Any verdict pronounced by the Khap Panchayat has no legitimacy and cannot be enforced by the state machinery. If the Khap Panchayat annuls the marriage of a couple in an inter-caste, interfaith, or same *gotra* marriage, the marriage will still be considered valid in India.[56],[57] Similarly, state institutions are bound to protect the couple. In *Asha Ranjan v State of Bihar and Other*,[58] the court pronounced that 'the choice of a woman in selecting her life partner is a legitimate constitutional right. It is founded on an individual choice that is recognised in the Constitution under Article 19,[59] and this right is not expected to succumb to the concept of class honour or group thinking'.[60] The judgment established that the right to choose a life partner is constitutionally guaranteed.[61] Therefore, the rights of indi-

---

[53]Marc Galanter, 'Snakes and Ladders: Suo Moto Intervention and the Indian Judiciary Symposium: Layers of Law and Social Order' (2014) 10 FIU Law Review 69.

[54]ibid 77.

[55]Johanna Bond, 'Honor as Property' (2012) 23 Columbia Journal of Gender and Law 202.

[56]Judgment in *Lata Singh* (n 158).

[57]Rakesh Rai, 'Inter-Caste Marriages and Reservation Policy in India: A Socio-Legal Study' (2016) 1 International Research Journal of Social Science & Humanities 56.

[58]*Asha Ranjan v State of Bihar and Other*.

[59]See the listing and wording of art 19(2) – (6ii).

[60]*Asha Ranjan* (n 172), para 48.

[61]Under the freedoms and provisions of art 24.

viduals guaranteed by the constitution and other laws of India are superior to communal rights. The concept of group honour or decision-making cannot deprive a person of the exercise of his or her rights; this reinforces the principles of gender equality,[62] namely non-discrimination, equality, and educational development, by extending rights that had been customarily reserved for men to women.

Social Support for Khap Panchayats

The Khap Panchayat still has great influence and enjoys the confidence of the people in many rural areas in India. The membership of the Khap Panchayat is voluntary and families voluntarily refer issues to the Khap Panchayat instead of approaching courts of law.[63] Different factors contribute towards the social support for the Khap Panchayat. One of the primary reasons is the delay in the pronouncement of judgments in courts of law.[64] Formal courts take years to decide on simple cases. The Khap Panchayat, however, delivers a verdict in a single hearing. Second, the institution has been in existence for centuries because of the trust that people invest in it.[65] Third, the Panchayat comprises village elders who are highly respected in society and to whom people can relate, unlike judges in courts of law.[66] Fourth, political parties support the Khap Panchayat system to protect their voter base. They are reluctant to

---

[62] UN Global Compact, 'Endorse the Women's Empowerment Principles' <https://www.unglobalcompact.org/take-action/action/womens-principles#:~:text=Take%20action%20across%20all%20seven,all%20women%20and%20men%20workers> accessed 26 July 2021.

[63] Bharadwaj (n 105).

[64] ibid.

[65] ibid.

[66] ibid.

act against these institutions, which may adversely affect their popularity. Manohar Lal Khattar, the Chief Minister of the State of Haryana extended his support to the institution, stating, 'They are like parents minding the children, and they take swift decisions on matters in which the courts are silent. Khap Panchayats consist of experienced members of the society and they make sensible decisions'.[67] This statement reflects the political patronage enjoyed by these institutions. Further, the complexity of the court system and the heavy expenses also contribute to the social support for the Khap Panchayat system.[68]

Problems in the Khap Panchayat System

The Khap Panchayat system contributes to several honour crimes. The institution provides social support and patronage to the perpetrators of honour crimes, as a result of which the accused in most such cases are absolved from the legal ramifications of the heinous crimes they commit. The diktats issued by the Khap Panchayat have resulted in the killings of hundreds of human beings, and numerous families have been compelled to commit crimes against their family members by the Khap Panchayat. These problems are explained in detail below.

Protection of Male Dominance

The Khap Panchayat is a patriarchal institution. To maintain male dominance, they impose restrictions on women's sexuality, which deprive women of the rights to express themselves

[67] Singh (n 123).

[68] Ashok Kumar Godara, 'Honour Killing and Role of Khap Panchayat: An Empirical Study' (2012) <http://14.139.58.147:8080/jspui/bitstream/123456789/47/1/07LLM12.pdf> accessed 26 July 2021.

and choose a life partner, and other fundamental rights.[69] In some areas, its diktats prohibit women from wearing jeans and/ or using mobile phones. These restrictions have limited women to the private sphere, and there is no representation of women in the Khap proceedings. The crimes committed in the name of honour are rooted in this patriarchal aspect of the Khap Panchayat.[70]

Violations of Indian Law

Audi Alteram Partem[71] is a significant principle of natural justice.[72] According to this norm, each party to a conflict is entitled to present their case, justify their claims, and deny allegations made by the other party. The right to be heard is protected by the Constitution and laws of India.[73] The *modus operandi* of the Khap Panchayat contradicts the principles of natural law. In its proceedings, parties are not given the opportunity to present their case or afforded the right to be heard. The members of the Khap Panchayat take into consideration the facts of the case and pronounce a judgment unilaterally. The parties to the conflict are not entitled to file an appeal against the Khap Panchayat's verdict in any other forum; the verdict is always final.[74] According to the analytical framework, Khap Panchayats do not provide tools to parties to mount a legal challenge against their verdicts.

---

[69]ibid.

[70]ibid.

[71]i.e. 'let the other side be heard as well'.

[72]John M Kelly, 'Audi Alteram Partem; Note' (1964) Natural Law Forum 103.

[73]ibid.

[74]Navin Kumar, 'Judicial Response Towards Khap Panchayat' (2013) 2 Journal of Global Research and Analysis 108.

Reinforcement of Illegal Cultural Practices

According to Article 13(1) of the Constitution of India, all customs, cultural practices, and traditions inconsistent with the fundamental rights in the Constitution are void.[75] The rights to marry, life, and express oneself are constitutionally protected.[76] The Khap Panchayat system enforces cultural practices that often deprive people of the exercise of their constitutional rights, which is a violation of legislative instruments like the Hindu Marriage Act 1955[77],[78] and the Special Marriage Act 1954.[79] Therefore, the Khap Panchayat is considered an illegal institution enforcing illegal practices whose decisions violate human rights.[80]

No Right to Plead

The Khap Panchayat system inflicts severe punishments on individuals who have violated its cultural norms and rules.[81] These punishments violate the domestic laws and provisions of international human rights instruments,[82] such as the UDHR,[83] ICCPR,[84] CEDAW,[85] and the United Nations Convention

---

[75]Constitution of India, art 13 (1).

[76]Constitution of India, art 21.

[77]The Hindu Marriage Act 1955.

[78]Rai (n 171).

[79]The Special Marriage Act 1954.

[80]Singh (n 24).

[81]Chesler (n 11).

[82]*Vikas Yadav* (n 128).

[83]Universal Declaration of Human Rights.

[84]International Covenant on Political and Civil Rights.

[85]The United Nations Convention on the Elimination of All Forms of Discrimination against Women.

against Torture.[86] The formal adjudicatory system also inflicts severe punishments such as the death penalty. According to a 2018, Amnesty International Report, India is 1 of 56 countries to retain the death penalty whereas 142 countries have abolished it in law and/or practice. The death penalty is imposed on those who commit very heinous crimes. The overall number of death sentences imposed by the sessions' court has decreased from 153 in 2016 to 77 in 2020.[87] Although courts of law do pronounce the death penalty in many cases, these sentences are commuted to life imprisonment or reduced punishments by higher courts.[88] The President of India is entitled to pardon those sentenced to death by commuting their punishments to life imprisonment. India has carried out 8 executions since 2000.[89] The comparison between the death penalties executed by the formal adjudicatory system and the cases of honour crimes committed with the aid of the Khap Panchayat indicates that the latter has been involved in the arbitrary killing of people.[90]

No Representation of Members of the Scheduled Castes

The Khap Panchayat includes members of the upper caste and no members from the scheduled castes.[91] The institution has

---

[86]The United Nations Convention against Torture.

[87]Abhishek K Singh, 'The Meandering Course of Death Penalty Sentencing in India: A Critical Analysis' (2015) 5 Nirma University Law Journal 19.

[88]Deutsch (n 32).

[89]Amanda Clough, 'Honour Killings, Partial Defences and the Exclusionary Conduct Model' (2016) 80 Journal of Criminal Law 177.

[90]Galanter (n 167).

[91]Kavita Kachhwaha, 'Khap Adjudication in India: Honouring the Culture with Crimes' (2011) 6 International Journal of Criminal Justice Sciences 297.

existed for centuries, especially in rural India. The members of the Khap Panchayat are self-proclaimed custodians of the norms and traditions of society.[92] They are very influential and have social support.[93] There is no representation of women, its proceedings do not provide an opportunity for women to be heard, and it enforces illegal cultural practices. It plays a crucial role in the commission of honour crimes by imposing social and economic sanctions on those who violate the norms and traditions of society.[94] The Khap Panchayat is a parallel adjudicatory system in India and has, therefore, been declared illegal by the courts of law in many judgments.[95] It has no legal standing under Indian law. The Khap Panchayat discriminates against the members of the scheduled castes and enforces ancient caste practices. Interactions with the members of the scheduled castes is considered equivalent to polluting the caste system; therefore, restrictions are imposed on inter-caste interactions. If anyone from a higher caste marries a member of a lower caste, it is considered a threat to the supremacy of the upper caste, and severe punishments are inflicted on the couple to prevent similar incidents in the future.[96] The discrimination and ill-treatment of the members of the scheduled castes are prohibited by the laws of India and constitute a violation of domestic[97] and international human rights laws.

---

[92]Bharadwaj (n 105).

[93]Ismail (n 13).

[94]ibid.

[95]See *Chandrapati* (n 154). Judgment in *Lata Singh* (n 158). *Asha Ranjan* (n 172), para 48.

[96]Singh (n 24).

[97]Constitution of India, art 15 (1).

Formal Adjudicatory System

This section analyses the legislative instruments and precedents set by the courts of law, applying the analytical framework to compare, contrast, and determine the efficacy of the formal and informal adjudicatory systems.

The Constitution of India

The Parliament of India[98] has not enacted a specific legislative instrument to deal with honour crimes within its jurisdiction, which is highly essential. The Constitution of India is the supreme law of the country. Part 3 of the Constitution provides protection to some of the most significant rights, known as the 'Fundamental Rights', to all inhabitants of India. The legislature is not entitled to abrogate or repeal any of the rights in Part 3 of the constitution through ordinary legislation. The Constitution also provides a mechanism for the enforcement of constitutional rights and empowers the higher judiciary to adjudicate upon cases involving the infringement of fundamental rights. Although the Constitution does not explicitly mention honour killings or crimes, the rights embodied in the constitution protect people against these crimes. Article 15 (1) states: 'All laws in force in the territory of India immediately before the commencement of this Constitution, in so far as they are inconsistent with the provisions of this Part, shall, to the extent of such inconsistency, be void'.[99] Subclause (a) of Clause 3 of Article

[98]The Union Legislature is called the 'Parliament'. It comprises the President and two Houses, known as the Council of States (Rajya Sabha) and the House of the People (Lok Sabha). Each House has to meet within six months of its previous sitting. A joint sitting of both Houses can be held in certain cases.

[99]Constitution of India, art 13 (1).

13 defines law as follows: 'Law includes any Ordinance, order, bye-law, rule, regulation, notification, custom or usage having in the territory of India the force of law'.[100] Article 13 imposes a legal obligation on all branches of the states to uphold the fundamental rights and any law, custom, usage, by-law, rule, regulation, notification, or practice prevalent in any part of India that infringes upon fundamental rights is void. Customs and practices that impose restrictions on women and make them the repository of honour are the causes of honour crimes. Therefore, they violate fundamental rights, such as the right to life and freedom of expression, and are illegal under Article 13 of the constitution.

Article 14 prohibits discrimination based on caste, colour, race, religion, and other distinguishing features and mandates equality before the law:[101] 'The State shall not deny to any person equality before the law or the equal protection of the laws within the territory of India'.[102] Article 15 (1) states, 'The State shall not discriminate against any citizen on grounds only of religion, race, caste, sex, place of birth or any of them'.[103] Another cause of honour crimes is the caste system.[104] Members of the upper castes consider themselves superior and discriminate against members of the lower castes. To maintain the supremacy of the upper caste, restrictions are imposed on the sexuality of women, and inter-caste and/or inter-religious mar-

---

[100]Constitution of India, art 13 (3) (a).

[101]Catherine A MacKinnon, 'Sex Equality under the Constitution of India: Problems, Prospects and Personal Laws' (2006) 4 International Journal of Constitutional Law 181.

[102]Constitution of India, art 14.

[103]Constitution of India, art 15 (1).

[104]S Murugananthan, '"Honour Killing" The Menace - A case study in Tamil Nadu' 2014 International Journal of Management Research and Social Science 1.

riages are prohibited. When a woman from an upper caste marries a man from a lower caste, the act is considered blasphemous and she is accused of polluting the caste and dishonouring her family. In such cases, members of the upper caste commit crimes of honour against the couple. Discrimination based on caste is a blatant violation of Articles 14 and 15 of the Constitution of India.[105] The Constitution also protects the right and liberty of all inhabitants of India. Article 21 states: 'No person shall be deprived of his life or personal liberty except according to the procedure established by law'.[106] Personal liberty refers to the right to make decisions for oneself, including the right to marry. Therefore, any restriction imposed to control the sexuality of women is a violation of Article 21. Similarly, honour killings, which deprive a person of his or her life, also violate Article 21. Any act that deprives a person of the right to life is a severe violation of the constitution and a crime under the laws of India. The constitution also protects the right to profess any religion. Article 25 (1) states that 'Subject to public order, morality, and health and the other provisions of this part, all persons are equally entitled to freedom of conscience and the right freely to profess, practice and propagate religion'.[107] Article 25 protects interfaith marriages,[108] which is a major reason for honour killings. Although the Constitution of India does not mention the words 'honour crime', Articles 13, 14, 15, 21, and 25 can be invoked to seek justice for victims of honour crimes.

---

[105]Surinder S. Jodhka and Jules Naudet, *Mapping the elite: power, privilege, and inequality* (1st edn OUP 2019)

[106]Constitution of India, art 21.

[107]Constitution of India, art 25 (1).

[108]MacKinnon (n 216).

The Hindu Marriage Act 1955

The centuries-old caste system prevalent in India is the most significant reason for honour crimes.[109] There are four main castes and many sub-castes and *gotras*. Those who fall outside the caste system are excluded from society and are referred to as '*Dalits*' or untouchables. Article 17 of the Constitution of India has abolished untouchability. However, the practice is still pervasive in many parts of India.[110] The members of the upper caste consider themselves superior to others and subject *Dalits* to inhuman treatment and discrimination. The caste system prohibits inter-caste marriages and imposes numerous restrictions particularly on the sexuality of women to prevent inter-caste marriages. As women's autonomy is considered a threat to the caste system, rules and regulations are enforced to control the sexuality of women and ensure compliance through the imposition of sanctions and penalties.[111]

The Hindu Marriage Act 1955 legalised inter-caste marriages.[112] Before the enactment of the law, inter-caste marriages were illegal and children from such marriages were considered illegitimate. In *Bai Kashi v Jamnadas Mansukh* (March 1912), the Bombay High Court held that marriage between the Brahmin widow Bai Kashi and Jamnadas, a Shudra was illegal,[113]

---

[109]See *Chandrapati* (n 154). Judgment in *Lata Singh* (n 158). *Asha Ranjan* (n 172), para 48.

[110]Tahira Karanjawala and Shivani Chugh, 'The Legal Battle against Domestic Violence in India: Evolution and Analysis' (2009) 23 International Journal of Law, Policy and the Family 289. Constitution of India, art 25 (1).

[111]Uma Chakravarti, 'Conceptualizing Brahmanical Patriarchy in Early India: Gender, Caste, Class and State' (1993) 28 Economic and Political Weekly 579.

[112]The Hindu Marriage Act 1955.

[113]*Bai Kashi v Jamnadas Mansukh*, 1912.

and the couple along with their children were deprived of the legal rights granted to same-caste couples and children under the law.[114] The Hindu Marriage Act 1955 legalised inter-caste marriages and protected inter-caste couples. Children from such marriages are also legitimate and entitled to all the rights granted to children of a valid marriage under the laws of India. Whereas the Hindu Marriage Act 1955 legalised inter-caste marriages, the incidence of such marriages is very low, reflecting the lack of social acceptance.[115] Ratna Devi, an upper-caste woman who married a Dalit man stated, 'For high-caste families, it is not only a crime but also a sin to marry someone of lower caste in India. I committed that sin and faced my family's wrath'. She and her husband were attacked by her family in the name of honour but timely intervention by the police saved their lives.[116] The victim's statement is a realistic reflection of the caste system and its rules, whose violations are considered a crime and truly evil.

The Scheduled Castes and Scheduled Tribes (Prevention of Atrocities) Act 1989

The marriage of upper-caste women with men from the scheduled castes is a prominent reason for honour crimes in India. Honour crimes committed against members of the scheduled castes are grounded in caste discrimination. Such individuals are not only discriminated against, but are also subjected to inhuman treatment. In many areas, members of the scheduled

---

[114]ibid.

[115]Rai (n 171).

[116]Umar Manzoor Shah, 'Caste-Driven Honour Killings Still Haunt India' (*UCA News*, 23 May 2019) <www.ucanews.com/news/caste-driven-honor-killings-still-haunt-india/85209#> accessed 26 July 2021.

castes are ostracised and deprived of fundamental rights and basic needs of life. The Parliament of India enacted the Scheduled Castes and Scheduled Tribes (Prevention of Atrocities) Act 1989 to eliminate atrocities committed against the members of the scheduled castes.[117] This Act resonated with Article 17 of the Constitution, which states: 'Untouchability is abolished and its practice in any form is forbidden. The enforcement of any disability arising out of untouchability shall be an offence punishable in accordance with law'.[118] Article 17 and the Act of 1989 integrated the members of the scheduled castes in Indian society and criminalised discrimination against them. The provisions of the Article and the Act may be invoked in honour crimes committed against members of the scheduled castes.

Udumalpet Shanker's murder is an example of an honour killing committed against a member of a scheduled caste to protect the honour of the family. Kausalya, who belonged to another backward class (OBC) community, and Shanker, who belonged to a scheduled caste community, got married without the approval of their families. Both were students in an engineering college. Kausalya's family was against this, as they considered marriage with a Dalit blasphemous. In the 10 months of their marriage, the couple received multiple threats before they were brutally attacked. Shanker reported serious injuries and Kausalya barely survived. The case was reported as an honour crime, and Kausalya's family members and the hired killers were apprehended. The lower court convicted her father and five others under the Prevention of Atrocities against Scheduled Castes and Scheduled Tribes Act (POA) and sen-

---

[117]The Scheduled Castes and Scheduled Tribes (Prevention of Atrocities) Act 1989.

[118]Constitution of India, art 17.

tenced them to death.[119] An appeal was filed in the Madras High Court against the decision of the lower court, which led to Kausalya's father and uncle being acquitted and the sentences of the other culprits being commuted. Kausalya intends to file an appeal against the judgment of the High Court with the Supreme Court of India.[120]

The Protection of Human Rights (Amendment) Act 2006

The Protection of Human Rights Act 1993[121] and the amendments made to it through the enactment of the Protection of Human Rights (Amendments) Act 2006[122] are significant legislative instruments in India. The provisions of the Act may be invoked in honour crimes, as they provide for the establishment of a National Human Rights Commission to investigate breaches of human rights. The commission has been empowered to conduct inquiries, examine witnesses, and give recommendations for the enforcement of international human rights

---

[119]Arun Janardhanan, 'Udumalpet Honour Killing: Shankar's Father-in-Law Acquitted by Madras HC' *The Indian Express* (Chennai, 22 June 2020) <https://indianexpress.com/article/cities/chennai/udumalpet-honour-killing-shankars-father-in-law-acquitted-by-madras-hc-6470569/> accessed 26 July 2021.

[120]Mohammad Imranullah S, 'Madras High Court Sets Aside Death Sentence Awarded to Prime Accused in 2016 Udumalpet Shankar Murder Case' *The Hindu* (Chennai, 22 June 2020) <www.thehindu.com/news/national/tamil-nadu/madras-high-court-sets-aside-death-awarded-to-prime-accused-in-2016-udumalpet-shankar-murder-case/article31887684.ece> accessed 26 July 2021.

[121]The Protection of Human Rights Act 1993.

[122]The Protection of Human Rights Act 1993 (with Amendment Act) 2006.

instruments in India[123] such as the ICCPR,[124] the ICESCR,[125] and the national legislative instruments for the protection of human rights.[126],[127] International legislative instruments contain provisions related to the protection of the life and liberty of people. The crimes committed in the name of honour are violations of the rights embodied in these international and national legislative instruments. Therefore, the provisions of this legislation may be employed in honour crimes, both for investigations and to implement measures to eliminate such crimes from society.[128]

The Protection of Women from Domestic Violence Act 2005

The Protection of Women from Domestic Violence Act 2005 may be employed in honour crimes. According to Section 2(f) of the Act:

> *A domestic relationship means a relationship between two persons who live or have, at any point of time,*

---

[123]National Human Rights Commission, India, 'Vision & Mission' <https://nhrc.nic.in/about-us/vision-and-mission> accessed 26 July 2021.

[124]International Covenant on Civil and Political Rights 1966.

[125]International Covenant on Economic, Social and Cultural Rights 1966.

[126]Such as The Protection of Human Rights Act 1993 (with Amendment Act 2006).

[127]The Protection of Human Rights (Amendment) Act 2019.

[128]Relis Tamara 'Unifying benefits of studies in legal pluralism: accessing actors' voices on human rights and legal pluralities in gender violence cases in India' (2016) 48 Journal of Legal Pluralism and Unofficial Law 354.

> *lived together in a shared household, when they are related by consanguinity, marriage, or through a relationship in the nature of marriage, adoption or are family members living together as a joint family.*[129]

Therefore, the honour crimes committed against women or their partners by their family members may fall into the category of domestic violence.[130] Section 3(a) defines domestic violence as any violence that 'harms or injures or endangers the health, safety, life, limb, or well-being, whether mental or physical, of the aggrieved person or tends to do so and includes causing physical abuse, sexual abuse, verbal and emotional abuse, and economic abuse'.[131] The definition of domestic violence is very broad and corresponds to acts often committed against women and their partners to protect the alleged honour of the family. Although the term 'honour crime' is not mentioned explicitly in the law, the provisions of these legislative instruments are invoked in honour crime cases, as honour crimes are often committed against women in the domestic sphere.[132] This act provides different remedies, such as compensation and custody.[133]

---

[129]Protection of Women from Domestic Violence Act 2005, s 2 (f).

[130]Manjeet Bhatia, 'Domestic Violence in India: Cases under the Protection of Women from Domestic Violence Act, 2005' (2012) 32 South Asia Research 103.

[131]Protection of Women from Domestic Violence Act 2005, s 3 (a).

[132]Karanjawala (n 225).

[133]ibid 305.

Relevant Provisions of the Indian Penal Code

The IPC is the most significant legislative instrument for criminal law in India. Its provisions not only define offences and the essential elements to prove them but also prescribe appropriate punishments. Section 299 of the IPC states:

> *Whoever causes death by doing an act with the intention of causing death or with the intention of causing such bodily injury as is likely to cause death, or with the knowledge that he is likely by such act to cause death, commits the offence of culpable homicide.*[134]

Similarly, Section 300 of the IPC states:

> *Except in the cases hereinafter excepted, culpable homicide is murder, if the act by which the death is done with the intention of causing death or if it has done with the intention of causing such bodily injury as the offender knows to be likely to cause the death of the person to whom the harm is cause.*[135]

The combined reading of Sections 299 and 300 indicates that there are two essential elements for murder–*actus reus* and *mens rea*. Any act resulting in the death of another person along with the intention to cause death is murder. Honour killings include both the *actus reus* and *mens rea*[136] and fall under the ambit of homicide amounting to murder. Therefore, if any person or group of individuals commit an act or inflict bodily injury on another person with the premeditated intention

[134]Indian Penal Code (IPC), s 299.

[135]Indian Penal Code (IPC), s 300.

[136]ibid.

of causing death, this act is considered murder under IPC Sections 299 and 300. The punishment for murder is prescribed under IPC Section 302: 'Whoever commits murder shall be punished with death or imprisonment for life, and shall also be liable to fine'.[137] Therefore, those convicted of honour killings should be punished with death or life imprisonment. If the accused does not cause the death of another person but causes bodily injury, they will be liable to the penalties prescribed in IPC Section 307:

> *Whoever does any act with such intention or knowledge and under such circumstances that, if he by that act caused death, he would be guilty of murder, shall be punished with imprisonment of either description for a term which may extend to ten years, and shall also be liable to fine, and if hurt is caused to any person by such act, the offender shall be liable either to imprisonment for life or to such punishment as is hereinbefore mentioned.*[138]

Section 307 is applicable to honour crimes that seek to cause the victim's death but instead resulted in bodily injury or harm. Honour crimes are generally committed by several people to protect the alleged honour of the family or community.[139] Therefore, Sections 34 and 35 of the IPC are also relevant and may be invoked against the group of individuals who commit honour crimes. Section 34 states: 'When a criminal act is done by several persons in furtherance of the common intention of all, each of such persons is liable for that act in the manner as if

---

[137]Indian Penal Code (IPC), s 302.

[138]Indian Penal Code (IPC), s 307.

[139]Ismail (n 13).

were done by him alone'.[140] All individuals who participate in a crime and share a common intention are guilty of the crime and will be liable for the consequences. Therefore, all members of the family or social group who participated in the commission of honour crimes will be liable for the consequences of the act. Section 107 of the IPC, which addresses abetment and conspiracy, is also relevant in honour crimes. It states:

> *A person abets the doing of a thing who instigates any person to do that thing; or engages with one or more other person or persons in any conspiracy for the doing of that thing if an act or illegal omission takes place in furtherance of that conspiracy and to the doing of that thing; or intentionally aids, by any act or illegal omission, the doing of that thing.*[141]

This Section may be invoked against those who instigate and support honour crimes. Many other sections of the IPC are relevant in honour crimes, including those related to conspiracy and the provisions related to harm and physical assault.

There is no specific law enacted by the Parliament of India to deal with honour crimes. However, the provisions of numerous legislative instruments are relevant. Therefore, in prosecuting honour crimes, the provisions of the Constitution of India for the protection of the fundamental rights of the inhabitants of India, the Hindu Marriage Act 1955, the Scheduled Castes and Scheduled Tribes (Prevention of Atrocities) Act 1989, the Protection of Human Rights (Amendment) Act 2006; the Protection of Women from Domestic Violence Act 2005, the IPC, and numerous other legislative instruments, such as the Indian Evi-

[140]Indian Penal Code (IPC), s 34.

[141]Indian Penal Code (IPC), s 107.

dence Act 1872,[142] and the Indian Majority Act 1857[143] may be invoked.

Judicial Precedents and the Role of Courts

The Indian judicial system comprises higher courts, including the Supreme Court, the High Courts, and many lower courts. The judicial system has played a significant role in addressing honour crimes and its judgments have been instrumental in the evolution of law in India. This section applies the three-tier criteria as an analytical framework to compare, contrast, and determine the efficacy of the formal and informal adjudicatory systems, by analysing the judgments of the Supreme Court and High Courts in India and the precedents set by the courts in honour crimes cases. The criteria for the effectiveness of the formal adjudicatory system will be determined by its ability to recognise transgression, the compatibility of judgments with the principles of gender equality, and whether such judgments can offer tools to redress or remedy crimes.

Manoj-Babli Honour Killing Case

The Manoj-Babli Honour Killing Case[144] is a landmark case in India,[145] as the courts prescribed capital punishment for the accused. Manoj and Babli lived in Karoran Village, Kaithal. They

---

[142]The Indian Evidence Act 1872.

[143]The Indian Majority Act 1875.

[144]*Chandrapati* (n 154).

[145]Anil Kumar Dubey, 'Honour Killing: The Socio-Legal Perspective and Judicial Approach' (2017) 17 International Journal of Research in Social Sciences 101.

belonged to the Banwala *gotra*, a Jat community, whose customs and norms prohibit marriage within the same *gotra*, as they consider members of the same *gotra* siblings. Manoj and Babli fell in love and eloped. When the news of their marriage became public, the village organised a Khap Panchayat to discuss the matter. The Khap Panchayat issued a diktat to annul the marriage and declare the couple brother and sister. The diktat pronounced by the Panchayat planned to isolate Manoj's family by imposing heavy sanctions on them. The couple was kidnapped by Babli's family members and brutally murdered.[146] The Karnal District Court passed a historic judgment in 2010. It prescribed death sentences to the perpetrators, who were brothers, uncles, and cousins, for the couple's murder.[147] The court handed down a life sentence to the leader of the Khap Panchayat for conspiracy to commit murder and seven years' imprisonment to the driver.[148] The district judge Vani Gopal Sharma's judgment stated:

> *This court has gone through sleepless nights and tried to put itself in the shoes of the offender. Khap Panchayats have functioned contrary to the constitution, ridiculed it, and have become a law unto themselves.*[149]

The court declared the Khap Panchayat illegal and repugnant to the Constitution of India.[150],[151] An appeal was filed against the judgment of the District Court before the Punjab and Haryana

---

[146] *Chandrapati* (n 154).

[147] ibid.

[148] ibid.

[149] ibid.

[150] ibid.

[151] Aakansha Katiyar and Nidhi Sri, 'Honor Killing - A Social Evil in Modern Indian Society' (2020) 2 International Journal of Juridical Studies & Research 8.

High Court, which commuted the death sentence of four convicts and acquitted the leader of the Khap Panchayat and the other convict, Satish.[152] The imposition of the death penalty was criticised by human rights groups,[153] who argue that it goes against the values of reformative justice and violates the dignity of human life.[154]

Marriage within the same *gotra* is legally permissible in India. Therefore, the marriage of the couple was legally valid. The decision of the Khap Panchayat to annul the marriage was a violation of Indian laws; therefore, the judgment of the District Court is significant.[155] It declared the Khap Panchayat contrary to the Constitution of India and re-established the right of the state. The judgment also indicated that the judicial system is the legitimate forum for the adjudication of cases, whereas the Khap Panchayat system contributes towards the commission of honour crimes. However, the judgment of the High Court undermined the historic judgment and allowed the release of the head of the Khap Panchayat. This move may have helped consolidate the position of the Khap Panchayat in rural India. This case may have been an opportunity to strengthen the principles of gender equality in India and provide redress for the crimes committed, but the High Court took

---

[152]*Chandrapati* (n 154).

[153]Carol S Steiker, 'No, Capital Punishment Is Not Morally Required: Deterrence, Deontology and the Death Penalty' (2005) 58 Stanford Law Review 751.

[154]Parliamentarians for Global Action, 'Campaign for the Abolition of the Death Penalty' <www.pgaction.org/ilhr/adp/?gclid=EAIaIQobChMIwIivz4K78QIVGIjVCh2_yAYvEAAYASAAEgKNEfD_BwE> accessed 26 July 2021.

[155]Shikha Dimri, 'Social Interventions into Anti-Social Actions: Critical Legal Analysis of Honour Killings' [2019] Bharati Law Review<https://papers.ssrn.com/sol3/papers.cfm?abstract_id=3759280> accessed 26 July 2021.

a step in the wrong direction, illustrating the difficulty the Indian judiciary faces in establishing progressive judgments against honour killings.

Lata Singh v The State of U.P. and Another

The Hindu Marriage Act 1955 and numerous other legislative instruments have legalised inter-caste marriages.[156] However, such marriages remain the primary cause of honour crimes.[157] In *Lata Singh v The State of U.P. and Another*,[158] the Supreme Court of India passed a significant judgment and upheld the legal validity of inter-caste marriages. Lata Singh, an adult woman, who was living in her brother's house, left the house on 2 November 2000 and married Bramha Nand Gupta at the Arya Samaj Mandir. Two days later, her brother lodged a missing person's report at a police station. The police arrested the sisters of Bramha Nand Gupta along with other family members on the charge of kidnapping. Lata Singh's brothers threatened their sisters-in-law, forcefully took possession of their property, and threatened the couple.[159]

The police and law enforcement agencies are legally bound to protect a couple in inter-caste marriages. However, in this case, Lata's brothers exploited the law. The police assisted the brothers and arrested the family members of the petitioner's in-laws. There were also ongoing proceedings against them in the subordinate courts.[160] Lata approached different women and

---

[156]Rai (n 171).

[157]See *Chandrapati* (n 154). Judgment in *Lata Singh* (n 158). *Asha Ranjan* (n 172), para 48.

[158]*Lata Singh* (n 158).

[159]ibid.

[160]ibid.

human rights organisations to intervene in the matter and sought protection for herself and her in-laws. She filed a petition before the Supreme Court under Article 32 of the Constitution of India. After taking into consideration the facts of the case, the apex court quashed the criminal proceedings instituted against Lata's in-laws and ordered the initiation of legal proceedings against her brothers. The Supreme Court passed a detailed judgment and declared the caste system a curse to the nation.[161] Justice Markandey Katju remarked, 'Honour killings are nothing but barbaric cold-blooded murder and no honour is involved in such killings'.[162] The court upheld that every adult individual is entitled to the right to choose their life partner and no one can interfere in the exercise of this right. It also upheld inter-caste marriages, stating 'Inter-Caste and Inter-religious marriages should be encouraged to strengthen the social fabric of society'.[163] This judgment may play a significant role in the protection of inter-caste marriages in India and change relevant social dynamics. It reflects the imperative role of the formal adjudicatory system in addressing violence in the name of honour, by breaking the traditional stereotypes prevalent in society and encouraging behaviour that promotes inclusiveness.[164] It recognises that honour killings are wrong, because it strengthens inter-caste and inter-religious marriages and proves that the prohibition is objectively wrong under national law, which strives towards strengthening the social fabric by creating a more equal India.[165]

---

[161] Judgment in *Lata Singh* (n 158).

[162] ibid.

[163] ibid.

[164] Clough (n 203).

[165] Jakob De Roover, 'Scheduled Castes vs. Caste Hindus: About a Colonial Distinction and Its Legal Impact' (2017) 13 Socio-Legal Review 22.

The State of U.P. v Krishna Master and Ors

Killings committed in the name of family honour fall under Section 300 of the IPC.[166] If the crime has been committed by a group of individuals in furtherance of a common intention, Section 34 of the IPC is applicable and each participant is liable for the consequences of the crime committed.[167] In The *State of U.P v Krishna Master and Ors*,[168] the court upheld that the killings committed in the name of honour also fall under the ambit of homicide amounting to murder and the penalty prescribed by the IPC for homicide amounting to murder has been prescribed by law. Therefore, the case was a significant precedent for all subordinate courts in India. Further, in this case,[169] the Supreme Court upheld the trial court's conviction and death sentence for three convicts who caused the death of six members of a family in an honour killing case in a village in Uttar Pradesh. Sontara, the daughter of the accused, had eloped with Amar Singh, son of Jhabbu Lal. The accused forced Jhabbu Lal and his neighbour Gulzari Lal to search for his daughter and ensure her return to the family. After receiving the threat, Jhabbu Lal and his neighbour visited different relatives looking for Amar Singh and Sontara, but failed to find any trace of the couple. At midnight, the three accused entered Gulzari Lal's house and started firing. Gulzari Lal, his wife, and three sons were badly injured. Upon hearing the gunshots, Jhabbu Lal and his wife left their house and took refuge in another house nearby. The three accused entered Jhabbu Lal's house. They did not find them there, but they found Baburam,

---

[166]Indian Penal Code (IPC), s 300.

[167]Indian Penal Code (IPC), s 34.

[168]*State of U.P. v Krishna Master & Ors.*, AIR [2010] SC 3071.

[169]ibid.

Jhabbu Lal's brother, and shot him dead. The incident resulted in the death of six people. The trial court convicted the three accused for the murder of six people, and handed down the death penalty and imposed fines. The verdict was challenged before the Allahabad High Court on a Criminal Appeal, which quashed the trial court's decision. An appeal was then filed before the Supreme Court against the judgment of the High Court. After taking the facts of the case into consideration, the Supreme Court restored the verdict of the trial court and set the judgment of the High Court aside. Justices H.S. Bedi and J.M. Panchal remarked:

> *There is no manner of doubt that killing six persons and wiping out almost the whole family on the flimsy ground of saving the honour of the family would fall within the rarest of rare cases and therefore, the trial court was perfectly justified in imposing the capital punishment on the respondents.*[170]

The judgment of the apex court recognised the gravity of honour crimes in the country and upheld the gravest punishment available under the law to discourage the commission of similar offences.[171] The proponents of strict punishments argue that it serves as a deterrent to prevent similar human rights violations; however, the opponents argue that reformative justice is more effective when the root causes of the crimes are addressed and that the imposition of strict penalties has failed to achieve any positive results.[172] Regardless of the merits of such

[170]ibid.

[171]Deler Singh and Dipali S Bhandari, 'Legacy of Honor and Violence: An Analysis of Factors Responsible for Honor Killings in Afghanistan, Canada, India, and Pakistan as Discussed in Selected Documentaries on Real Cases' (2021) 11 SAGE Open 215824402110223.

[172]ibid.

derivative arguments, it is clear that the judgment recognises the extreme wrong committed in such instances of violence and provides the best remedy available to the victims.[173] The analytical framework indicates that the application of the most serious punishment by the formal adjudicatory system reflects that the courts of law considered honour crimes the most heinous crimes and wanted to prevent their occurrence by setting precedents. The Khap Panchayat, in contrast, justifies honour killings through traditions and customs.[174]

Bhagwan Dass v the State of Delhi

The Supreme Court of India convicted the accused of honour killing in *Bhagwan Dass v the State of Delhi.*[175] The victim, Seema, the daughter of the accused, was married for three years and then left her husband. She was alleged to have had an adulterous relationship with her uncle. Her family members accused her of ruining the family's honour and her father strangled her to death with an electric wire. The trial court convicted the accused,[176] who filed an appeal before the High Court against the conviction. The High Court upheld the conviction. The accused appealed before the Supreme Court. After considering the facts of the case, the Supreme Court dismissed the appeal and upheld the conviction, stating thus:

> *In our opinion honour killings, for whatever reason, come within the category of rarest of rare cases de-*

---

[173]ibid.

[174]Mayuri Gupta, 'Strengthening the Backward Class: Role of National Commission for Backward Classes' (2018) 8 GNLU Journal of Law Development and Politics 93.

[175]*Bhagwan Dass v State of Delhi* [2011] 9 May.

[176]ibid.

> *serving death punishment. It is time to stamp out these barbaric, feudal practices, which are a slur on our nation. This is necessary as a deterrent for such outrageous, uncivilised behaviour.*[177]

The judgment of the apex court is significant because it recognised that honour killings are a national issue and not criminal acts alone, but also grave violations of the fundamental rights of human beings. Therefore, the State is duty-bound to prevent the commission of such offences and uphold the dignity of human beings.[178] Thus, the Indian judiciary is playing a strong role in the evolution of the law, based on human rights, gender equality, and the desire for justice for victims of grave crimes.[179] In this case, the Supreme Court justified the death penalty for the convicts of honour killings, which it considered heinous crimes.

To discourage their commission, Indian courts have pronounced the most severe punishments available under the law. The language used by the court indicates that it considers the death penalty a deterrent in honour crime cases.[180] India is 1 of the 56 countries in which the death penalty is legalised; however, in most cases, the death penalty is changed into life imprisonment and other forms of reduced punishment.[181] The President of India is empowered by the Constitution under Article 72[182] to grant pardons, reprieves, and respites, or to remit punishments, or to suspend, remove, or commute the sentence

---

[177]ibid.

[178]ibid.

[179]Singh and Bhandari (n 286).

[180]Singh (n 169) 263.

[181]Kunal Ambasta, 'An Unclear Empiricism: A Review of the Death Penalty India Report' (2017) 13 Socio-Legal Review 130.

[182]The Constitution of India, art 72.

of any person who has been sentenced to death. Thus, the courts of law have pronounced the death penalty on rare occasions alone.[183]

Shakti Vahini v Union of India

Shakti Vahini v Union of India[184] is a recent Indian case involving honour crimes. Shakti Vahini, a women's right organisation advocating for the legal rights of women in India, was authorised by the National Commission for Women to conduct research on honour killings in Haryana and western Uttar Pradesh.[185] Their findings highlighted the growing prevalence of honour crimes in the regions examined. The organisation filed a petition before the Supreme Court under Article 32 of the Constitution of India[186] seeking direction from the court to the central and state governments to take preventive measures in order to eliminate honour crimes. The petitioner requested the central and state governments to submit a National Plan of Action and State Plans of Action, respectively, to address honour crimes in their respective jurisdictions.[187] The plans were to include directions for other measures such as the establishment of a special cell for couples and prosecution of the perpetrators of honour crimes.[188] The respondent (i.e., the Union of India), stated that 'The Prohibition of Interference with the Freedom

[183]Dhananjay Kashyap, 'Death Penalty in India' (2013) Asian Journal of Legal Studies 70.

[184]*Shakti Vahini v Union of India* AIR [2018] SC 1601.

[185]Satnam Singh Deol, 'Honour Killings in Haryana State, India: A Content Analysis' (2014) 9 International Journal of Criminal Justice Sciences 192.

[186]Constitution of India, art 32.

[187]*Shakti Vahini* (n 298), Writ Petition (Civil) N0. 231 of 2010.

[188]ibid.

of Matrimonial Alliance Bill' was under legislative consideration, indicating that because the matter falls within the current jurisdiction, the centre is bound to take the states on board and that many states had responded positively to the bill.[189]

The Supreme Court of India passed a historical and detailed judgment in the case, recognising the severity of honour crimes and their serious repercussions for the greater good of the country, issuing directions to the central and state governments to take preventive, punitive, and remedial measures in order to build a strong system to combat and eliminate honour crimes.[190] Justice Dipak Misra quoted French philosopher and thinker Simone Weil: 'We don't live in a world in which there exists a single definition of honour anymore, and it's a fool that hangs on to the traditional standards and hopes that the world will come around him'.[191] The judgment cited some of the most important honour crime judgments, such as *Asha Ranjan v The State of Bihar*:[192] 'The choice of a woman in choosing her life partner is a legitimate constitutional right. It is founded on the individual choice that is recognised in the constitution under Article 19,[193] and such a right is not expected to succumb to the concept of class honour or group thinking'.[194] The Supreme Court recognised that the right to choose a partner is constitutionally protected and guaranteed and that no one is entitled to interfere in the exercise of this right. Insofar as this right applies equally to women, the court will further the principles of gender equality in Indian rights. This judgment may

---

[189]ibid.

[190]*Shakti Vahini* (n 298).

[191]ibid.

[192]*Asha Ranjan* (n 172).

[193]Constitution of India, art 19.

[194]Rankin (n 69).

even result in the enactment of a specific legislative instrument to address honour crimes, as mentioned by the Union of India before the Supreme Court. It also reflects the influence of the court of law in policymaking and the enactment of the law. A National Plan of Action may result in prompt and collaborative action by all stakeholders towards taking holistic measures to eliminate honour crimes in the country.

Sanjay v The State of Haryana

In this case, three teenagers, Bodhi alias Vinod, Suman, and Budha alias Satish, were brutally killed in the name of honour by the father of a girl named Suman, Jita Ram. He claimed that the two boys had enticed his daughter to elope from their home, which affected his reputation in society negatively and brought dishonour to his family. To reclaim their lost honour, he murdered the three teenagers. Initially, he confessed to the crime, but later refused to admit his guilt. However, the evidence provided by the prosecution established his guilt. The trial court convicted Jita Ram, and Sanjay, Budha's first cousin, for the murder of the three teenagers. The trial court sentenced them to life imprisonment and imposed a fine of Rs. 5000 each. The convicts appealed against the trial court decision before the High Court and challenged the conviction. The High Court dismissed the appeal and upheld the judgment of the trial court. It held that the prosecution had proved the case beyond all reasonable doubt.[195] The conviction pronounced by the trial court and the High Court's dismissal of the appeal set an important precedent. Haryana has one of the highest numbers of honour crimes in India. The Khap Panchayat has a strong presence in the state and plays an important role and offers patronage to the

[195]*Sanjay v. State of Haryana*, Crl. in the High Court of Punjab and Haryana at Chandigarh Appeal No. 662- DB of 2005.

perpetrators of honour crimes.[196] Society accepts the orders of the Khap Panchayat. The judgments of the Trial and High Courts not only set a precedent for subordinate courts to convict perpetrators of honour crimes, but also played a role in changing the social structure in the area because perpetrators are generally protected against the legal consequences of their acts, which results in a larger number of honour crimes.[197] Therefore, the imposition of penalties on perpetrators can discourage honour crime cases in the future.

The analysis of the precedents of the higher courts of India in the Manoj-Babli Honour Killing Case, *Lata Singh v the State of UP and Another, The State of UP v Krishna Master and Ors, Bhagwan Dass v the State of Delhi, Shakti Vahini v Union of India,* and *Sanjay v State of Haryana* indicates that the judiciary plays a significant role in contrasting honour crimes by identifying the offences committed, bolstering the principles of gender equality, and providing redress to victims.

Indian courts have recognised that the right to choose a partner is a constitutional right and that no one is entitled to interfere with the exercise of this right. Similarly, the judgments of these courts have affirmed that inter-caste marriages, marriages within the same *gotra*, and inter-religious marriages are legally recognised in India and that no institution including the Khap Panchayat is entitled to annul such marriages. The courts have also played a role in the prevention of honour crimes by directing federal and state governments to take preventive, remedial, and punitive measures to eliminate the crime by holding the perpetrators accountable. Without the courts of law, the perpetrators of honour crimes may not have to face the consequences of the crimes they commit, as the Khap Panchayat system pro-

---

[196] Ismail (n 13).

[197] Singh and Bhandari (n 286).

tects them. This sense of accountability may discourage people from committing similar offences. Honour crimes were previously justified in the name of tradition, and violence committed in the name of honour was not considered a crime. Now, they have been declared serious societal crimes for which the courts will and do offer redress to victims. The judgments of the courts impose penalties on the perpetrators and the executive actions the penalties. Similarly, the government is bound to protect couples in inter-caste, inter-religious, and inter-*gotra* marriages and prevent them from coming to any harm. The judgments of the higher courts play a role in the evolution of law as seen in *Shakti Vahini v Union of India,*[198] where the Union mentioned that a bill is under consideration. These judgments have the potential to change the social dynamics and punishments imposed on those who commit honour crimes can serve as deterrence for others.[199] Therefore, the role of the Indian judiciary has truly been commendable.

Problems in the Formal Adjudicatory System in India

The analysis of the provisions of relevant legislative instruments and the precedents of the higher courts in honour crimes shows that the formal adjudicatory system strives to protect the rights of the people of India. The judgments pronounced by the higher courts have contributed to the evolution of laws related to honour crimes. However, there are some problems in the legislative and judicial systems of India in this regard. To make

---

[198]*Shakti Vahini* (n 298).

[199]Valerie Wright, 'Deterrence in Criminal Justice, Evaluating Certainty vs. Severity of Punishment' (2010) The Sentencing Project.

the formal adjudicatory system more effective, reliable, and accessible, it is essential to address its challenges.

The Defence of Grave and Sudden Provocation

Honour killings are premeditated and planned murders that fall within the ambit of Section 300 (homicide amounting to murder) of the IPC. However, in most honour crime cases, the defence of grave and sudden provocation is invoked to mitigate the sentence of the convicts of honour killings. Exception 1 to Section 300 of the IPC states, 'Culpable homicide is not murder if the offender, while deprived of the power of self-control by grave and sudden provocation, causes the death of the person who gave the provocation or causes the death of any other person by mistake or accident'.[200] The section indicates that there are three elements to claim the defence of grave and sudden provocation – the provocation was sudden, grave, and resulted in the loss of self-control.[201] Sudden provocation means that the provocation was unexpected. The interval between the homicide and provocation is minimal. If the accused committed the homicide after a lapse of reasonable time, the defence of sudden provocation will not hold. The second requirement is that the provocation is grave. To determine the gravity of the provocation, the court will administer an objective test,[202] and take into consideration multiple factors such as the social context, financial standing, and educational background in order to determine whether a reasonable man would be likely to lose self-control as a result of such provocation under the given circumstances. If the answer is in the affirmative, the court will

[200]Indian Penal Code (IPC), s 300, Exception 1.

[201]ibid.

[202]*Nanavati* (n 98).

classify it as a grave provocation. The third requirement is the loss of self-control. If the court is satisfied that provocation is sudden and grave, it will assume the loss of self-control. All three elements must be satisfied.

In *K.M. Nanavati v State of Maharashtra,*[203] naval officer K.M. Nanavati murdered businessman Prem Ahuja. It was an honour crime, in which the accused murdered the victim for having an illicit relationship with his wife. The accused claimed the defence of grave and sudden provocation to mitigate his sentence.[204] In this case, although the court admitted that the defence of grave and sudden provocation may be justified in honour crimes, the plea of the accused was rejected because too much time had passed. However, in many honour killings, the defence of grave and sudden provocation has been granted and convicts have successfully mitigated their sentences.[205]

The Delay in the Registration and Solemnisation of Marriages

In India, court marriages are governed by the Special Marriage Act 1954, which applies to all people without any discrimination on the basis of caste, religion, and race. Although the provisions of the Act empower adults to enter into a valid marriage, the procedure established under the Act for the registration and solemnisation of valid marriages can contribute towards the commission of honour crimes. A couple intending to get married has to file a notice of intended marriage with the

---

[203]ibid.

[204]Gautam Narasimhan, 'Revisiting S.105 of the Indian Evidence Act, 1872' (1998) 10 Student Advocate 52.

[205]*Nanavati* (n 98).

marriage registrar:[206] 'The Marriage Officer shall cause every such notice to be published by affixing a copy thereof to some conspicuous place in his office'.[207] After receiving the notice, the marriage registrar will publish it and invite objections if any. Individuals have 30 days to object to the marriage. If there is no valid objection, the marriage is formalised and enjoys legal protection. This procedure often results in serious repercussions for couples that seek to get married without the approval of their parents. When a notice is published, the intention of the couple becomes public and they become vulnerable to social pressure without any legal protection. In many cases, family members of women commit honour crimes after the publication of the notice.[208] In other cases, the couple is subjected to violence and forceful means are used to prevent the solemnisation of their marriage. In some cases, the families of women force them to enter into marriages that comply with their social norms. Therefore, the Special Marriage Act has been heavily criticised.[209]

The Need for a Legislative Instrument Specifically Addressing Honour Crimes

The provisions of numerous legislative instruments are invoked in addressing honour crimes. The Constitution of India, the IPC, Human Rights Protection Act 2006, and other legislative instruments are relevant. However, the nature of honour crimes and killings demands a specific legislative instrument. Existing

---

[206]Special Marriage Act 1954.

[207]The Special Marriage Act 1954, cl 2, s 6.

[208]Rubi Talukdar and Maithili Chaudhury, 'The Special Marriage Act 1954' (2020) 57 Psychology and Education 1007.

[209]Kanika Gupta, 'Gender Based Violence: Honour Killings' (2014) 8 Asian Journal of Development Matters 178.

laws do not address the specific nature of honour crimes, which have a particular socio-political context.[210] The application of the three-tier analytical framework indicates that the nature of honour crimes differs from that of other crimes. Society assists law enforcement agencies in the investigation of criminal cases and there is a consensus on the inimical ramifications of crimes on society. However, the nature of honour crimes is different.[211] These crimes are justified in different communities, wherein the community and family members encourage perpetrators to commit honour crimes. After the commission of the crime, they all unite to conceal evidence and protect the accused from legal consequences. Even where the law enforcement agencies investigate and convict individuals for the commission of an honour crime, the crime itself is appreciated and considered an act of courage, unlike other crimes, which attract condemnation from society. Therefore, existing legislative instruments may not be able to fully cater to the peculiar dynamics of honour crimes.[212]

This peculiar nature demands a specific law with due consideration for the social, economic, cultural, and other relevant factors motivating the commission of honour crimes. The laws enacted for the abolition of dowry and sati have proven effective in eliminating these social evils. The provisions of different laws that have been invoked in honour crimes cases have been exploited by perpetrators, who plead grave and sudden provocation to mitigate their sentence. This claim, if accepted by the courts, puts the victims of honour crimes at a greater disadvantage. Thus, the enactment of a specific honour crime

---

[210] Singh (n 50).

[211] Katja Luopajarvi, 'International Accountability for Honour Killings as Human Rights Violations' (2004) 22 Nordisk Tidsskrift for Menneskerettigheter 2.

[212] ibid, 11.

legislation is necessary against honour crimes, bearing in mind the dynamics of honour crimes in the country and addressing the challenges of honour killings that are prevalent in many parts.

Low Representation of Women in the Judicial System

The patriarchal system and dominance of males in society are among the many root causes of honour crimes. It is essential to promote gender sensitisation to address honour crimes. Gender sensitisation is a basic requirement to understand the sensitive needs of a particular gender, whilst examining attitudes and beliefs that are inherently regressive. An inclusive judicial system with an equal representation of men and women will be more considerate to gender sensitivities, as women who experience the same social context can relate to the experiences of other women.[213] Similarly, owing to cultural barriers and segregation, in many areas, women are not comfortable about openly discussing issues with men; therefore, it is most likely that women victims of honour crimes may be more comfortable in the company of women and may openly discuss things they may hesitate to discuss with men.[214] Gender sensitisation demands equal representation of both genders in all spheres of life. The judiciary, as the custodian of rights, plays a very important role in the adjudication of honour crimes. Therefore, it

[213] Antal Csanad, 'Legal Transplantation in India Colloquium' (2009) 2009 Jura: A Pecsi Tudomanyegyetem Allam- es Jogtudomanyi Karanak tudomanyos lapja 185.

[214] Arachana Parashar, 'Gender Inequality and Religious Personal Laws in India India's Left Behind' (2008) 14 Brown Journal of World Affairs 103.

is crucial to have equal representation of both genders in the judicial system to promote gender sensitisation. K.K. Venugopal, the Attorney General of India, stated:

> *There are only 80 women judges out of the total sanctioned strength of 1,113 judges in the High Courts and the Supreme Court across India ... Out of these 80 women judges, there are only two in the Supreme Court, and the other 78 are in various High Courts, comprising only 7.2 per cent of the total number of judges.*[215]

Women are not well represented in the Indian judiciary.[216] Both genders should have equal representation to better address gender-based violence and honour crimes.

Low Reporting and Conviction Rates

Three factors contribute to the low reporting and conviction rates of honour crimes. In many cases, honour crimes are committed because of social pressure. The perpetrator is highly regarded in society and the crime is treated as an act of courage to protect family honour. Therefore, in most cases, honour crimes are not reported to law enforcement agencies, except for grave offences.[217] A specific legislative instrument dealing with the different aspects of honour crimes and their socio-cultural

---

[215]G Ananthakrishnan, 'Improve Representation of Women in the Judiciary, Sensitize Judges: AG to SC' *The Indian Express* (3 December 2020) <https://indianexpress.com/article/india/improve-representation-of-women-in-judiciary-sensitise-judges-ag-to-sc-7079925/> accessed 26 July 2021.

[216]ibid.

[217]Jodhka and Naudet (n 219).

dynamics may enhance reportage. Second, the courts in India are burdened with cases, with hundreds of thousands currently pending before the judiciary.[218] Third, honour crimes have social support, as does the Khap Panchayat, which often protects perpetrators by concealing material evidence. Thus, the conviction rates are very low.[219] The lack of social support contributes to low conviction rates as eyewitnesses refuse to give testimonies, and material evidence is concealed to protect the accused.

The most critical problems in India's formal adjudicatory system include the defence of grave and sudden provocation, the procedure for the registration and solemnisation under the Special Marriage Act 1954, the absence of a specific legislative instrument to address honour crimes, low representation of women in the judiciary and other law enforcement agencies, and low reportage and conviction rates. Although the law contains provisions that can apply in addressing honour killings and other forms of grave violence, the diversity of honour crimes are not embodied in these laws. The formulation and enactment of a specific law, that embodies honour crimes substantively and nationally, will broaden the parameters of formal adjudication. The enactment of a specific law would: (i) recognise transgressions; (ii) be compatible with principles of gender equality; and (iii) offer tools to redress or remedy honour crimes via criminal prosecution and sentencing. This may change the situation of honour crime adjudication, as a specific law would be multi-pronged, but specifically directed at recognising and providing a tool to remedy honour crimes.

---

[218]ibid.

[219]Sumedha Pal, 'Conviction Rates Remain Low, While Encounter "Justice" Increases' (*NewsClick*, 2019), <www.newsclick.in/conviction-rates-remain-low-while-encounter-justice-increases> accessed 26 July 2021.

CHAPTER 3
FORMAL AND INFORMAL HONOUR CRIME ADJUDICATORY SYSTEMS IN PAKISTAN

Pakistan accounts for one-fifth, the highest number, of documented cases of honour killings in the world.[1] Although the government of Pakistan does not issue any official account of the total number of honour killings and other forms of violence committed in the name of honour, it is estimated that approximately 1,000 honour killings are committed in the country every year.[2] According to a report by *Dawn*, a national newspaper in Pakistan, in the province of Sindh, a total of 769 individuals were killed in the name of honour between 2014 and 2019. Among them, 510 were female and 259 were male.[3] Other provinces of Pakistan, including Punjab, Khyber Pakhtunkhwa, and Balochistan, have reported killings and oth-

---

[1] Human Rights Country Report of 2018.

[2] Honour Based Violence Awareness Network <http://hbv-awareness.com/statistics-data/#Pakistan> accessed 26 July 2021.

[3] Imtiaz Ali, '510 Women, 259 Men Fell Prey to "Honour" Killings during Five Years in Sindh' *Dawn* (19 February 2020) <www.dawn.com/news/1535295> accessed 26 July 2021.

er forms of violence in the name of honour. Most honour crimes are committed against women, who are considered an embodiment of honour. Therefore, this study specifically focuses on honour crimes committed against women. The statistics[4] indicate that honour crimes, particularly killings, constitute a very serious problem in Pakistan. Although both men and women are subject to violence in the name of honour,[5] violence against the latter is more widespread.[6]

Communal values, which are considered more important than individual rights and freedoms, are very strong in Pakistan.[7] The community and society have set certain standards and parameters that all residents must abide by. If an individual violates standard practice, the social forces use various coercive means to ensure compliance. These social and quasi-legal forces include the Jirga or community council, which exists mainly in rural areas of Pakistan. Individual rights and freedoms are severely restricted in a communal society,[8] where individual rights are subordinate to community values. Individual choices are discouraged and homogeneous behaviour is encouraged. If an individual commits an act that violates communal values, it is a threat to the existence of the community. To uphold community values and the importance of community life, individuals are subject to various forms of violence. Even families have been known to use various means to ensure ad-

---

[4]Indian Penal Code (IPC), s 300, Exception 1.

[5]ibid.

[6]ibid.

[7]Raza Anjana 'Mask of Honor-Causes behind Honor Killings in Pakistan' (2006) 12 Asian Journal of Women's Studies 88.

[8]Simon S Laham and others, 'Emotional and Behavioural Reactions to Moral Transgressions: Cross-Cultural and Individual Variations in India and Britain' (2010) 45 International Journal of Psychology 64.

herence to community values, including violence against their members.[9]

Communal values, combined with the patriarchal system in Pakistan, challenge women significantly, wherein rules dictate their lives. One of the social norms is the concept of honour. In Pakistan, women are believed to embody the honour of family and society.[10],[11] To protect the honour of the family, a woman has to follow established practices and norms, and any deviation from them is condemned. Women who violate established practices are accused of bringing dishonour to the family, and society imposes a responsibility on men to protect the honour of the family.[12] If a woman deviates from these practices, the men in their families and society with the support of other women can employ forceful and coercive means and commit honour killings and other forms of violence against the 'deviant' woman to restore the honour of the family or the community. Nida Kirmani, Associate Professor of sociology at Lahore University said, 'Honour crimes are committed as a way of policing or disciplining women, girls, men, and boys who are seen to be violating these rules'.[13]

The primary objective of honour crimes is to ensure compliance with traditional norms that promote communal values and

---

[9]Maliha Zia Lari, 'A Pilot Study on Honour Killings in Pakistan and Compliance of Law' [2011] Aurat Publication and Information Service Foundation <www.af.org.pk/pub_files/1366345831.pdf> accessed 26 July 2021.

[10]Chesler (n 11).

[11]Kaushal (n 47).

[12]Chakrabarti (n 25).

[13]Shah Meer Baloch, 'Pakistan Authorities Records a Dozen Cases of Honour Killing in a Fortnight' *The Guardian* (17 May 2019) <www.theguardian.com/global-development/2019/may/17/pakistan-authorities-record-a-dozen-cases-of-honour-killing-in-a-fortnight> accessed 26 July 2021.

prioritise communal rights over an individual human being. These norms often come in direct conflict with the liberal concept of individual human rights, which originated in the West following the philosophy of Edmund Burke and the French Revolution. These values confine women to the private sphere, discouraging their participation in private life. In rural Pakistan, the institutions of Jirga and Panchayat exert a very strong influence on people's lives.[14] They reinforce the subordinate position of women and control their behaviour. Women in urban areas are comparatively better off, as they enjoy the freedom of movement, are better educated, and are aware of their legal rights when compared to their rural counterparts.[15] However, honour-based crimes including honour killings are reported in both urban and rural areas and in every social strata and part of Pakistan.

Informal Honour Crimes Adjudicatory Systems in Pakistan

Pakistan's informal court system comprises jirgas, which prevail in Pashtun-dominated areas, and the Panchayat, which prevails in other parts of Pakistan (especially Sindh and Balochistan). These systems have a long history. They have evolved and consolidated their position in society over long periods of time. Owing to centuries-old traditions, both systems enjoy social support. However, there is evidence that the institutions have been involved in flagrant human rights violations,

[14]Tilmann J Roder, *Non-State Justice Institutions and the Law* (1st edn, Springer 2015).

[15]Uzma Panhwar and others, 'Critical Analysis of the Impact of Job on the Social Status of Women in Pakistan' (2017) 8 Journal of Education and Practice 17.

especially in cases of honour crimes. This section examines the role of the Jirga and Panchayat in the context of honour crimes.

The Jirga

The Jirga is widespread in the Pashtun-inhabited tribal provinces of Khyber Pakhtunkhwa and Balochistan in Pakistan. Over the centuries, the Pashtuns/Pakhtuns have developed a code of conduct that governs the behaviour of their members (known as Pashtunwali/Pakhtunwali). All members of the Pashtun tribal areas are obliged to abide by this code of conduct. One of the most important aspects of Pashtunwali is the Jirga system, a traditional assembly of tribal leaders that performs various tasks, including resolving disputes. This system exerts great influence in the tribal areas and enjoys social support, with all the decisions of the Jirga being fully enforced with the help of social support.[16] The Pakistani legislature recognised the importance of the Jirga in the Alternative Dispute Resolution Act 2017,[17] and integrated it into the formal adjudicatory system. This Act sought to limit the jurisdiction of the Jirga and promote just principles in its proceedings. It laid down rules to regulate the conduct of the Jirga and the prescribed limits for the cases decided by it.[18] The Jirga is only entitled to resolve civil disputes and has no jurisdiction over criminal cases.[19] However, the government does not authorise the Jirga, which is regulated by traditions and local practices

[16]Yasmeen Aftab Ali, 'Understanding Pashtunwali' *The Nation* (6 August 2013) <https://nation.com.pk/06-Aug-2013/understanding-pashtunwali> accessed 26 July 2021.

[17]The Alternate Dispute Resolution Act 2017.

[18]ibid, para 4.

[19]ibid, para 11.

and does not act in compliance with the Alternate Dispute Resolution Act 2017. The Jirga has been criticised for committing and enabling grave human rights violations.[20] The Alternate Dispute Resolution Act 2017 has limited the jurisdiction of the Jirga to very specific cases. However, owing to centuries-old traditions and the influence of the Jirga in some areas of Pakistan, the Act has not been successful in curtailing its power. Therefore, state institutions must ensure the enforcement of the laws enacted by the legislative bodies and ensure that the informal bodies do not transgress the limits set by the law. The application of the analytical framework suggests that legislative instruments may be effective in regulating the conduct of informal adjudicatory bodies. However, this is not possible without an effective enforcement mechanism.

The Panchayat

The Panchayat refers to the village council or community organisations in rural Punjab and Sindh. Similar to the Jirga, the elders of the village gather in one place and perform various tasks such as settling disputes among villagers. The Panchayat goes back centuries and is part of the customs and culture of rural Pakistan. Its decisions are enforced by the locals.[21] It plays an important role in protecting and enforcing customary law practices to regulate the conduct of its members.[22] However, it has been subject to criticism by human rights organisa-

---

[20]Chesler (n 11).

[21]ibid.

[22]Neha Ansari, 'Biased/Unbiased: The Parallel Justice System in Rural Pakistan - A Close Scrutiny' *The Express Tribune* (Karachi, 26 February 2014) <https://tribune.com.pk/story/676185/biasedunbiased-the-parallel-justice-system-in-rural-pakistan-a-close-scrutiny> 26 July 2021.

tions[23] and civil society members for its involvement in honour crime cases and violations of national and international human rights instruments.[24]

Role of the Jirga and Panchayat Systems in Honour Crime Cases

The Jirga and the Panchayat have been accused of providing support in cases of honour crimes.[25] As both institutions have their roots in cultural practices, they enforce cultural norms. Those who violate these practices are considered threats to the institutions. Therefore, the Jirga and Panchayat employ various means to ensure compliance with the customs and traditions of their areas. Many cultural practices in the tribal areas in the form of Pashtunwali and in rural areas are based on patriarchal norms that discriminate against women and govern their behaviour.[26] These practices are based on the subordination of women and aim to promote male supremacy and violate national and international norms.[27] A tradition that confines women within the walls of the home and prevents them from participating in public life violates, for example, their freedoms

[23]Human Rights Commission of Pakistan, 'HRCP Annual Report 2015' [2015] <http://hrcp-web.org/hrcpweb/hrcp-annual-report-2015/> accessed 26 July 2021.

[24]ibid.

[25]Sanya Dhingra, (2017), 'Revenge Rape, Honour Killings as "Justice": Pakistan's Problematic Jirgas Get More Power (*The Print*, 2017) <https://theprint.in/report/revenge-rape-honour-killings-justice-pakistan-jirgas/13878/> accessed 26 July 2021.

[26]Allah Nawaz Robina, 'Jirga and Panchayat as the Precursor to Honour Killing in Pakistan' (2020) <www.qurtuba.edu.pk/thedialogue/The%20Dialogue/15_1/15_1_12.pdf> accessed 26 July 2021.

[27]ibid.

of movement, work, etc. Therefore, the Jirga and Panchayat have been heavily criticised by human rights groups and civil society organisations.[28],[29] Women's rights activist and columnist Marvi Sirmed said, 'Jirgas are extremely misogynist, patriarchal, anti-poor and anti-minority'.[30] The Jirga and Panchayat consider women property and are implicated in serious human rights violations. These institutions are usually made up of the elite and maintain their power through the subordination of women and other weak groups.[31] She also added, 'There is an elite capture across Jirgas, and they are invariably dominated by conservative religious leaders [who] influence great control in these tribal councils and sanctioned the judgment passed by the council'.[32]

The Jirga has sanctioned numerous murders in the name of honour. One such case is the Kohistan case.[33] In 2011, a video emerged from Kohistan, a conservative tribal area in northern Pakistan, showing a few women named Bazeegha, Sereen Jan, Begum Jan, Amina, and Shaheen singing and clapping. The video also shows a man dancing with them, and another man filming them. They were at a wedding and the women were seen wearing the traditional dress. They were not involved in anything that could be considered inappropriate. However, gossiping and singing by girls is considered taboo in Kohistan and

---

[28]US State Department, 'Pakistan 2019 Human Rights Report' (2019) <www.state.gov/wp-content/uploads/2020/03/PAKISTAN-2019-HUMAN-RIGHTS-REPORT.pdf> accessed 26 July 2021.

[29]Reema Omer and Sheila Varadan, 'Authority without Accountability: The Search for Justice in Pakistan' [2013] International Commission of Jurors.

[30]Robina (n 359).

[31]Chesler (n 11).

[32]Matthew (n 134).

[33]*The State v Mohammad Umar Khan, Saeer and Sabir* [2012] PCR 9376.

other tribal areas, where women have to stay at home and are not allowed to show themselves in public. In 2012, Afzal Kohistani, the brother of the two boys seen in the video, approached law enforcement authorities in Pakistan, claiming that the girls in the video were murdered by their families on the orders of the local Jirga.[34] He also accused one of the local religious leaders of having approved the murder of the women because of their so-called offence against tribal culture.[35] Afzal Kohistani claimed that his brothers' lives were in danger and asked for protection for them. These allegations gained national and international attention and the Supreme Court sent a commission to Kohistan to investigate the case. After the commission submitted a report, the case was closed.[36] Later, the case was reopened and some of the male members of the women's families were arrested. The Supreme Court demanded that the women in the video appear in court, but these orders were not obeyed.[37] The locals claimed that the court's orders went against their cultural norms, which forbid the appearance of women in public places, including the court. Even the country's highest court had failed to ensure the appearance of women in its premises.[38] This reflects the failure of state institutions to execute the orders of the court and establish the right of the state. This case resulted in the murder of nine innocent individuals, including Afzal Kohistani, the man who risked his

---

[34]ibid.

[35]Asad Hashim, 'How a Pakistani whistle-blower was killed for "Honour"' (*Al Jazeera*, 2019) <www.aljazeera.com/features/2019/3/26/how-a-pakistani-whistle-blower-was-killed-for-honour> accessed 26 July 2021.

[36]ibid.

[37]ibid.

[38]ibid.

life to seek justice that the courts could not grant.[39] It reflects the power and influence of the Jirga in the tribal areas of Pakistan, which consider themselves above the law. It also shows how complex the issue is, how evidence is concealed, and how perpetrators escape legal consequences with the support of the Jirga.

The Panchayat in rural Punjab and Sindh also contributes to various forms of violence against women. The case of Mukhtaran Mai is one of the most famous cases in which the crime was committed on behalf of the Panchayat.[40] A Mastoi tribal council ordered the gang rape of Mukhtaran Mai in 2002. It pronounced the judgment on the allegations made by the Mastoi tribe against the younger brother of Mukhtaran Mai,[41] who was accused of having a sexual relationship with a woman of the Mastoi tribe and bringing dishonour to their tribe.[42] To restore the honour of the tribe and take revenge, the Panchayat ordered the gang rape of Mukhtaran Mai.[43] She was raped by several men in the village of Meerawalla. It was later discovered that the accusation against her brother was fabricated by the Mastoi tribe.[44] Mukhtaran Mai approached the law enforcement authorities and filed charges against the perpetrators.

---

[39]Rashid Javed, 'Afzal Kohistani Murder: Family Ends Protest Following Protracted Negotiations with the Police' *Dawn* (Pakistan, 7 March 2019) <www.dawn.com/news/1468197> accessed 26 July 2021.

[40]Lahore High Court Multan Bench Multan (Judicial Department) Criminal Appeal No 60/2002.

[41]ibid.

[42]ibid.

[43]ibid.

[44]Ben Farmer, 'Mukhtar Mai, Pakistan's Gang Rape Survivor, Vows She Will Not Back Down as She Fights on for Justice' *The Telegraph* (Islamabad, 10 March 2019) <www.telegraph.co.uk/global-health/women-and-girls/mukhtar-mai-pakistans-gang-rape-survivor-sets-school-fights/> accessed 26 July 2021.

The anti-terror court sentenced 6 of the 14 defendants to death.[45] Four were convicted of rape and eight were released. Two Panchayat members were also convicted by the court. The perpetrators appealed to the Lahore High Court, which overturned the lower court's verdict and acquitted five of the six perpetrators and commuted the death sentence of one accused to life imprisonment.[46] Mukhtaran Mai's subsequent appeal to the Supreme Court was dismissed. She filed a review petition against the rejection of the appeal by the Supreme Court.[47] This case highlights the flaws in both the formal and informal adjudicatory systems.

The Panchayat and Jirga treat women as the property of the family and use them to take revenge on a family or tribe.[48],[49] The decisions of the Panchayat reflect an arbitrary system in which the powerful sections of society impose punishments on weak groups without giving them the opportunity to justify their cases. Mukhtaran Mai's case highlights the gaps in Pakistan's judiciary, where a victim of gang rape ordered by a Panchayat has to wait decades for justice. This case also reflects the flaws in both the formal and informal adjudicatory systems. The gang rape was committed on the orders of the Panchayat. When the victim approached the formal adjudicatory mechanism to seek justice, it failed to deliver. The case has been lingering on for years, and justice delayed is justice denied. There are numerous cases where the Panchayat system

---

[45] ibid.

[46] ibid.

[47] Mazna Hussain, 'Take My Riches, Give Me Justice: A Contextual Analysis of Pakistan's Honour Crimes Legislation' (2006) 29 Harvard Journal of Law & Gender 223.

[48] Nazish Brohi, *Women, Violence and Jirgas: Consensus and Impunity in Pakistan* (NCSW 2017).

[49] Chakrabarti (n 25).

has imposed similar punishments on members of vulnerable groups – especially women – and most of these cases are not even reported to the law enforcement agencies.[50]

Legal Status of Informal Systems in Pakistan

The Alternative Dispute Resolution Act 2017 recognised the Panchayat and Jirga as mechanisms for out-of-court settlements,[51] which enable the peaceful resolution of civil disputes by mutual consensus among the parties involved in the conflict. The Act facilitated the work of the overburdened courts and ensured that justice was accessible at the grassroots. It provides that the parties to a conflict may refer the matter to a neutral third party upon a mutual agreement.[52] If either party to the dispute refuses to refer the matter to a neutral party, including the Jirga and Panchayat, then the court will decide the matter.[53] This Act integrated these systems into the formal legal system of Pakistan and limited their jurisdiction.[54] They could offer arbitration, mediation, conciliation, and other forms of alternative dispute resolution in minor civil matters. The appointment of the Panchayat and Jirga would depend on the voluntary con-

[50]Usman Shahid, 'Inquest into Justice of the Pakistani Customary "Panchayat Justice System" in the context of the International Human Rights Law' (Master's thesis, University of London 2012) <https://core.ac.uk/download/pdf/13120138.pdf?repositoryId=99> accessed 26 July 2021.

[51]The Alternate Dispute Resolution Act 2017.

[52]ibid, art 3.

[53]ibid, art 11.

[54]ibid, s 3(1) Schedule of Jurisdiction.

sent of the parties.[55] The Panchayat and Jirga have no jurisdiction over criminal cases, including honour crimes. The Alternative Dispute Resolution Act has been criticised by human rights groups,[56] who argue that the Jirga and Panchayat contribute towards the commission of honour crimes and pronounce barbaric penalties. Instead of taking measures to eliminate these systems, the Act grants them legal recognition for peaceful settlements in civil cases, such as disagreements between the community members on minor issues, which can make minorities more vulnerable before the elite-administered systems. Some members of the Legislative Assembly opposed this bill.[57] The act limited the jurisdiction of the Jirga as a dispute resolution body, and the disputes that can be referred to these bodies will be minor ones of a civil nature rather than criminal cases.

The National Commission on the Status of Women (NCSW), a prominent women's rights organisation in Pakistan, approached the Supreme Court with a request for an explanation on the legal status of the Panchayat and Jirga and challenged their power to adjudicate on various matters.[58],[59] The Supreme Court held that the Jirga and Panchayat are contradictory to the international commitments undertaken by Pakistan with the

---

[55]Criminal Law (Amendment) Act 2004 Paragraph 12.

[56]Matthew (n 134).

[57]'Alternate Dispute Resolution Bill Approved' *Dawn* (Islamabad, 19 January 2017) <www.dawn.com/news/1309323> accessed 26 July 2021.

[58]Brohi (n 382).

[59]Majida Razvi, *A Study of Formal and Parallel Legal Systems Prevalent in Pakistan* (National Commission on Status of Women 2011) <www.ncsw.gov.pk/SiteImage/Downloads/A%20Study%20of%20Formal%20and%20Parallel%20Legal%20Systems%20Prevalent%20in%20Pakistan.pdf> accessed 26 July 2021.

ratification of CEDAW,[60] ICCPR,[61] and several other instruments.[62] The two institutions work as parallel legal systems and violate Articles 4, 8, 10-A, and 175(3) of the Constitution of Pakistan, which affirm the right of individuals to be dealt with in accordance with the law, that laws inconsistent with or in derogation of fundamental rights are void, and the right to fair trial, respectively. Therefore, these systems are not entitled to function as courts or judicial bodies.[63],[64],[65] However, the Supreme Court is unlikely to call for the complete elimination of the Jirga and Panchayat, as long as they operate within the limits prescribed by law and play their role in settling minor civil disputes. The Alternate Dispute Resolution Act 2011 and the Supreme Court judgment in the NCSW petition confirmed that the Jirga and Panchayat have very limited jurisdiction,[66] and no jurisdiction to adjudicate upon criminal offences[67] in parallel to the formal court system. Therefore, Jirga and Panchayat pronouncements in honour crime cases are illegal and constitute a violation of the legislative instruments and precedents of Pakistani High Courts.

[60]Convention on the Elimination of All Forms of Discrimination against Women New York 1979.

[61]International Covenant on Civil and Political Rights.

[62]*Servai v State of Tamil Nadu.*

[63]Hussain (n 380).

[64]Brohi (n 381).

[65]Shahid (n 383).

[66]*Arumugam* (n 156).

[67]ibid.

Social Support for the Panchayat and Jirga Systems

While there is no law enforcement agency to implement the verdicts of the panchayats and jirgas, the two institutions continue wield great influence in many parts of Pakistan and enjoy the trust of the people. The orders issued by these institutions are obeyed by the public,[68] most of whom prefer to approach these institutions over national courts, for reasons such as speedy adjudication.[69] These institutions resolve disputes in a single sitting and the decision is final, unlike in the case of courts. People in rural areas cannot afford the cost of formal adjudication. The concept of honour is ambiguous.[70],[71] In some quarters, even clapping or laughing in public is considered inappropriate as it transgresses standard behaviour and is not in line with the cultural practices of the majority of Pakistanis.

Problems in the Jirga and Panchayat Systems

This section applies the three-tier analytical framework to compare, contrast, and determine the efficacy of the formal and informal adjudicatory mechanisms. It analyses the flaws in the informal system and establishes how the formal system is more effective in recognising transgressions and remedy honour crime cases.

---

[68]Chakrabarti (n 25).

[69]Advocate Barakatullah and Ahmad Sajid Imran, 'Jirga System in Pakhtun Society: An Informal Mechanism for Dispute Resolution' (2013) 5 Pakistan Journal of Criminology 45.

[70]Laham (n 341).

[71]D'Lima (n 15).

Violation of Constitutional and Other Legislative Instruments in Pakistan

Article 10-A of the Constitution of Pakistan protects the right to a fair trial.[72] Many other legal instruments provide access to justice for every individual and offer a modus operandi to be followed by the courts in deciding the case. One of the most important aspects of a fair trial is the opportunity to be heard. It is also a principle of natural justice that parties to a dispute are given adequate opportunity to appear before a court and substantiate their claims or contest allegations. The right to be heard has been protected by the Constitution of Pakistan and the courts of law in Pakistan have passed judgments[73] indicating that every person has the right to justify or deny the charges brought against them by another party, irrespective of the gravity of the crime committed; and that no one can be denied this fundamental right. However, the Jirga and Panchayat deny parties these fundamental rights. In these institutions, the elders assemble and pronounce a verdict after considering the facts. The parties are not entitled to legal representation in asserting their claims. The verdict is final and there is no forum to challenge it. This is a violation of the constitutional provisions and the principles of natural justice.

---

[72]Constitution of the Islamic Republic of Pakistan, art 10-A.

[73]Hina Hafeezullah Ishaq, 'The Right to Fair Trial: Better Late than Never' (2014) 1 LUMS Law Journal 96.

The Lack of Female Representation in the Panchayat and Jirga

The Jirga and Panchayat lack female representation, which disproportionately affects women.[74] They treat women as property, and women are often exchanged. Punishments such as gang rape, forced suicide, and harassment are imposed on women of particular families or tribes to avenge insult. In other cases, the female members of a family or tribe have to answer for the acts of their male family members. The systems also discriminate against women in cases where both men and women are guilty. Women face harsh punishments while the accused men escape punishment.

Imposition of Inhuman Punishments

The Jirga and Panchayat have passed numerous judgments that undermine the dignity of the people. For example, Mukhtaran Mai was raped on the orders of the Panchayat, which sent her home naked. She was stripped in front of the villagers and gang raped with the intention of humiliating and causing her irreparable loss of dignity. The Constitution of Pakistan and numerous other national and international human rights instruments[75],[76],[77],[78] prohibit degrading punishments and protect the dignity of all human beings under all circumstances. Pakistan has also undertaken an international commitment by signing

---

[74]Shaikh Abdur Rashid, 'Jirga System and Women's Rights' (2021) <www.pakistantoday.com.pk/2021/03/12/Jirga-system-and-womens-rights/> accessed 26 July 2021.

[75]Universal Declaration of Human Rights 1948, art 1.

[76]International Covenant on Civil and Political Rights 1966.

[77]International Covenant on Economic, Social and Cultural Rights 1966.

[78]Convention on the Elimination of All Forms of Discrimination against Women 1979.

the Convention against Torture, and Other Cruel, Inhuman or Degrading Treatment or Punishment (CAT),[79] which enjoins it to uphold its obligation to prevent torture or cruel and degrading punishments from occurring on its territory by any means available to it. Therefore, Pakistan must ensure that the Constitution, national laws, and international obligations are respected and inhumane practices committed in the country on the orders of the Jirga and Panchayat are prevented.

Promotion of Illegal Cultural Practices

Customs, traditions, and norms contradictory to the rights embodied within Articles 8 to 28 of the Constitution of Pakistani are void.[80] However, the cultural practices enforced by the Jirga and Panchayat institutions, such as the confinement of women to the private sphere, the arbitrary verdicts of the village council and the crimes committed in the name of honour, violate constitutional provisions[81],[82] and other laws that protect the fundamental rights of people living in Pakistan.

Formal Adjudicatory System for Honour Crimes in Pakistan

The formal adjudicatory system in Pakistan reflects patriarchal values. The legislature of Pakistan has enacted pro-women legislation including anti-honour killing laws.[83] However, they have failed to improve the situation of women. The Pakistani

[79]The Convention against Torture, and Other Cruel, Inhuman or degrading treatment or Punishment (CAT).

[80]Constitution of Pakistan, art 8.

[81]ibid, arts 8- 28.

[82]ibid.

[83]The Criminal Law (Amendment) Act 2004.

judiciary has also given contradictory verdicts in cases of honour crimes. This chapter analyses Pakistan's formal and informal judicial systems in relation to honour crimes. The formal adjudicatory mechanism in Pakistan includes the laws enacted by the federal and provincial legislative bodies, the interpretation of the legislative instruments by the courts of law, and the adjudication of cases by the judicial system of Pakistan. This section applies the three-tier analytical framework to the formal adjudicatory mechanism in Pakistan.

Legislations Related to Honour Crimes in Pakistan

The legislature of Pakistan has enacted a specific legislative instrument[84] to deal with honour crimes within its jurisdiction. Various other legal instruments protect women's rights and discourage honour crimes without explicitly mentioning the term 'honour crime'. Some relevant legal provisions that may be invoked in cases of honour crimes are discussed below.

The Constitution of Pakistan

Articles 8 to 28 of the 1973 Constitution protect the Fundamental Rights of the citizens of Pakistan. These rights are constitutionally protected and the Pakistani legislature is not entitled to abrogate or override the fundamental rights by simple legislation. They are therefore considered the most important rights. The Constitution of Pakistan also provides a mechanism for the enforcement of fundamental rights and empowers the higher

---

[84]ibid.

judiciary to ensure the enforcement of constitutional rights. Article 184 (3) of the Constitution reads as follows:

> *Without prejudice to the provisions of Article 199, the Supreme Court shall if it considers that a question of public importance with reference to the enforcement of any of the Fundamental Rights conferred by Chapter I of Part II is involved have the power to make an order of the nature mentioned in the said Article.*[85]

If there is any violation of the fundamental rights embodied in the constitution and it becomes a matter of public importance, any individual or group may invoke the original jurisdiction of the Supreme Court of Pakistan to ensure the enforcement of fundamental rights.[86] Article 199 of the Constitution empowers the Supreme Court in each province to enforce fundamental rights within its territorial jurisdiction. Thus, if there is a violation of fundamental rights, the party with *locus standii* can invoke the writ jurisdiction of the High Court and seek the guarantee of fundamental rights.[87] Although the rights enshrined in the Constitution protect people against honour crimes, they do not specifically mention the term ‘honour killings’ or ‘honour crimes’. Some of the relevant articles of the Constitution that provide protection against honour crimes are provided below:

Any law or any custom or usage having the force of law, in so far it is inconsistent with the rights conferred by this chapter shall to the extent of such inconsistency, be void.[88]

This article obliges all organs of the state to uphold and guarantee the fundamental rights enshrined in the Constitution.

---

[85]Constitution of Pakistan, art 184 (3).

[86]As per the common law concept of Original Jurisdiction.

[87]Constitution of Pakistan, art 199.

[88]ibid, art 8 (1).

If a law contradicts the rights enshrined in the Constitution, it has no legal standing. Similarly, cultural practices and usages that are contradictory to fundamental rights are void.[89] The constitution protects the right to life,[90] prevents extrajudicial killings,[91] and protects the right to equality without any discrimination.[92] Customs and norms based on discrimination against women that enforce gender stereotypes, such as honour crimes, are repugnant to the constitution,[93] as they violate fundamental rights. Anyone who defends or upholds these cultural practices, thus, violates a constitutional provision. 'No person shall be deprived of life or liberty save in accordance with law'.[94] The right to life is the most important. It is the responsibility of the state to ensure its protection. No one can interfere with the rights to life and liberty of another person unless the act is sanctioned by law.[95] As perpetrators who commit honour killings deprive a person of their right to life, they blatantly violate this constitutionally protected right. The right to liberty protects the fundamental freedom and choice of an individual.[96] However, in Pakistan, individual rights are very restricted.[97] When a person chooses a partner for marriage, they are effectively exercising their right. Crimes committed in the name of honour to enforce a particular dress code or deprive a

[89]ibid.

[90]ibid, art 9.

[91]ibid, art 4 (2) (a).

[92]ibid, art 25 (2).

[93]ibid.

[94]ibid, art 9.

[95]ibid, art 4 (2) (a).

[96]ibid, art 4 (2) (b)-(c).

[97]ibid, arts 4 (1) to 4 (2).

person of the opportunity to decide for themselves, including the right to marry, violate constitutionally protected rights.

The Constitution protects the freedom of movement:

> *Every citizen shall have the right, subject to reasonable restrictions prescribed by law in the public interest, to remain, enter and move freely throughout Pakistan and to reside and settle in any part of Pakistan.*[98]

The gender-neutral wording of the article means that men and women have the right to move from one place to another. Cultural practices that restrict the movement of women and confine them within the boundaries of their homes to protect the so-called 'honour' of the family contradict Article 15. The Constitution of Pakistan also prevents discrimination on the basis of sex and grants equal rights to both sexes:

> *All citizens are equal before the law and are entitled to equal protection of the law. There shall be no discrimination on the basis of sex.*[99]

As honour crimes reinforce patriarchal norms based on discrimination and the subordination of women, they violate these constitutional provisions.[100]

[98]ibid, art 15.

[99]ibid, art 25-A.

[100]National Commission for Human Rights, 'A Study on Honour Killings in Pakistan and Recommendatory Checks through Law' [2019] The Office of the Chairman, National Commission for Human Rights, Government of Pakistan <https://nchr.gov.pk/wp-content/uploads/2019/01/Final-Report-Honour-Killing.pdf> accessed 26 July 2021.

Section 300 of the Pakistan Penal Code

After Partition, provisions were adopted from the IPC 1860, which was enacted by the British. Section 300 states that 'except in the cases hereinafter excepted, culpable homicide is murder if the act which the death is caused is done to cause death'. However, Exception 1 to Section 300 states, 'Culpable homicide is not murder if the offender, while deprived of the power of self-control by grave and sudden provocation, causes the death of the person who gave the provocation or causes the death of or other people by mistake or accident'.[101] The plea of grave and sudden provocation under Exception 1 of Section 300 has been used to mitigate sentences for honour killings. Pakistani courts have passed numerous judgments, recognising the plea as a relevant factor in these cases.[102]

Qisas and Diyat Ordinance

The PPC is the most important penal law in the country. Although it is based on customary law, during the Zia regime, various provisions were amended and replaced by new ones, such as the integration of Hudood, and Qisas and Diyat Ordinance, as part of its Islamisation policy.[103] Religion was used as a means to legitimise rule in the country: 'Historically, every time a government felt threatened or insecure, it resorted to Islamic rhetoric in the hope of gaining legitimacy and prolonging its existence'.[104] The Zia regime introduced many new laws and amended existing ones to satisfy the public. However, the

---

[101] Pakistan Penal Code (PPC), Exception 1 to s 300.

[102] Nicole Pope, *Honour Killings in the Twenty First Century* (1st edn, Palgrave Macmillan 2012).

[103] Charles H Kennedy, 'Islamization and Legal Reforms in Pakistan, 1979-1989' (1990) 63 Pacific Affairs 62.

[104] Professor Ishtiaq Ahmed cited in Hussain (n 311).

changes in the law and the integration of religious laws had negative consequences for the country, especially for women. The Zia regime held that all laws in the country must be in accordance with Islamic precepts and declared that any law that contradicts Islamic principles is null and void.[105] To ensure conformity with Islamic precepts, the Zia regime laid the foundation for Shariat Courts, which operate in parallel with the common law courts in Pakistan. With the establishment of these courts, many laws were challenged on the grounds that they did not conform to Islamic precepts.[106] In *Federation of Pakistan v Gul Hassan and Others*,[107] the Shariat Court found that some provisions of the PPC contradicted Islamic precepts and directed the government to amend its provisions; this led to the introduction of Qisas and Diyat Ordinance in 1990.[108]

The concept of *qisas* refers to equal retribution or treatment.[109] It has its roots in Islamic law and, as an Islamic conception of justice, defines just retribution as an eye for an eye, a nose for a nose, and a tooth for a tooth. However, *Diyat* refers to the compensation of the victim or the victim's heirs.[110] According to these concepts, the heirs of a victim are entitled to waive the punishment of the accused in return for or refusal of compensatory payment.[111] With the inclusion of Qisas and

[105]Raiz Hussain, 'Islamization: An Analysis of Religious, Political and Social Change in Pakistan' (1985) 21 Middle Eastern Studies 263.

[106]Shahbaz Ahmad Cheema, 'Non-Repugnancy Decisions of the Federal Shariat Court of Pakistan: An Analysis of Politico-Legal Ramifications' (2020) 7 LUMS Law Journal 48.

[107]*Federation of Pakistan v Gul Hassan and Others* PLD 1989 SC 633.

[108]Qisas and Diyat Ordinance, 1990.

[109]Stephanie Palo, 'A Charade of Change: Qisas and Diyat Ordinance Allows Honour Killings to Go Unpunished in Pakistan' [2008] U.C. Davis. Journal of International Law and Policy 93.

[110]ibid.

[111]ibid.

Diyat in the laws, Pakistan's penal codes empowered the legal heirs of the victim to claim compensation and waive punishment for the accused. If the family members of the accused exercised their right to diyat, the judicial authorities had to acquit the accused.[112] The inclusion of Qisas and Diyat in the law changed the nature of crimes. Previously, the state was responsible for prosecution and a crime was considered an offence against the state.[113] However, the Qisas and Diyat Ordinance resulted in the privatisation of the legal process and justice, and placed them in the control of the victim's legal heirs.[114] The ordinance empowers the '*wali'* of the victim to claim the right to *qisas* and *diyat.*[115] Section 299 (m) of the PPC defines *wali* as 'a person entitled to claim *qisas*'[116] whereas Section 305 reads, 'In case of a *qatl*, the *wali* shall be the heirs of the victim, according to personal law or the government, if there is no heir'.[117] This section has taken away the power of the government and empowers the *wali* of individuals to demand *qisas or diyat* from the accused. The *wali* as an institution is based on the discrimination and subordination of women and is empowered to control the behaviour of women; in cases of crimes committed against them, including honour crimes, the *wali* is empowered by law to remit or mitigate the punishment of the perpetrators.[118]

---

[112]Evan Gottesman, 'The Reemergence of Qisas and Diyat in Pakistan' (1992) 23 Columbia Human Rights Law Review 433.

[113]ibid.

[114]ibid.

[115]Alam Qadeer, 'The Qisas and Diyat Law in Pakistan: Prosecution of the Offence of Murder' (2019) 58 Islamic Studies 551.

[116]Pakistani Penal Code, s 299(m); emphasis added.

[117]Pakistani Penal Code, s 305; emphasis added.

[118]As per the common law concept of Original Jurisdiction.

Section 309 of the PPC provides, 'In the case of *Qatl-e-amd*, an adult *wali* may, at any time and without any compensation, waive his right to *qisas*'.[119] The *wali*, being a family member, commutes the sentence or forgives the perpetrator even in cases where they have a substantial interest in the accused. In the Samia Sarwar case,[120] for example, the brother, who was the *wali* of the victim, exercised his right and forgave the perpetrators. Samia Sarwar was married and had two children. She belonged to an educated and wealthy family in Peshawar. She was married to her cousin at a young age and wanted to divorce him. She told her parents that her husband was physically and mentally abusing her. Her parents were not in favour of divorce as it was considered taboo. After constant rejection, she eloped to Lahore with Nadir Mirza, an army officer. They stayed in a hotel for a few days and ran out of money. When the family discovered her whereabouts, Nadir Mirza returned to the army and Samia sought refuge in a women's shelter in Lahore. She took the help of two prominent lawyers to obtain a divorce from her husband and seek safety from her parents.[121] Her mother contacted her while she was in Lahore. On the day of her murder, Samia waited for her mother at her lawyer's office. Her mother was supposed to bring the divorce papers, but she came with an armed man. Samia was shot dead in her lawyer's office in front of her lawyers and other witnesses. Her mother fled the scene and the gunman was shot dead by the police. The case attracted national and international attention and various

---

119Pakistani Penal Code, s 309; emphasis added.

120Pope (n 435).

121Palo (n 442).

media houses covered it.[122,123] Even in this high-profile case, the perpetrators were acquitted by the court. Samia's brother, her legal heir, forgave the perpetrators. In this and several other cases, the victim's *wali* had the right to seek compensation to forgive the accused or to waive punishment of the accused without compensation.[124]

The Qisas and Diyat Ordinance resulted in serious repercussions for the criminal justice system, particularly in honour crimes cases.[125,126] The Constitution of Pakistan and other laws have imposed a duty on the state to protect the rights of its inhabitants, including their right to life. Therefore, murder, assault, or any other crime is considered a crime against the state and the state prosecutes the criminal. However, the Qisas and Diyat Ordinance absolves the state from prosecuting the accused and places the responsibility on the family members. In most cases, family members are involved in the commission of honour crimes with the support and consent of other family members, including the heirs of the victim. In such cases, the punishment for the accused is remitted by the legal heirs or *wali* and the accused walks free without being reprimanded. These Islamic legal concepts hinder justice for victims, as they prevent both the recognition of a wrong committed and the victim's right to redress. Insofar as they apply to honour killings with female victims, they contradict the principles of gender

---

[122]Kathy Gannon, 'A Woman Sacrificed for Honor of Her Family' *LA Times* (Lahore, 9 July 2000) <www.latimes.com/archives/la-xpm-2000-jul-09-mn-50070-story.html> accessed 26 July 2021.

[123]U Ali, 'Cover Story: Murder in the Name of Honour' (*Newsline*, August 2016) <https://newslinemagazine.com/magazine/murder-name-honour/> accessed 26 July 2021.

[124]Pope (n 435).

[125]Qadeer (n 448).

[126]ibid.

equality. The application of the analytical framework indicates that the provisions of qisas and diyat have complicated the situation and created hurdles for victims to seek justice before the courts of law. To improve the formal adjudicatory system, these flaws must be addressed.

The Criminal Law (Amendment) Act 2004

The Criminal Law (Amendment) Act 2004[127] is a significant development in anti-honour crime legislation. With this act, the Parliament of Pakistan introduced significant changes in the PPC against honour crimes. For the first time in the legal history of Pakistan, the law defined honour crimes by inserting a new clause under Section 299 of the PPC which reads thus: '[An] offence committed in the name or on the pretext of honour means an offence committed in the name or on the pretext of *karo kari, siyah kari* or similar other customs or practices'.[128] The definition of honour crimes is broad and includes any offence or act of violence committed to protect or restore the so-called honour of the family. This definition has also recognised that honour crimes have their roots in the cultural norms and customs of society. The Criminal Law (Amendment) Act 2004 increased the penalties for honour crimes and amended Section 311 of the PPC,[129] which now reads thus:

> *Notwithstanding anything contained in Section 309 or Section 310, where the wali does not waive or compound the right of qisas or if the principle of Fasad-fil-arz, the court may, having regard to the facts and cir-*

[127]The Criminal Law (Amendment) Act 2004.

[128]Pakistani Penal Code, s 299; emphasis added.

[129]Pakistani Penal Code, s 311.

> *cumstances of the case, punish an offender against whom the right of qisas has been waived or compounded with death or imprisonment for life or imprisonment of either description for a term of which may extend to fourteen years as ta'zir.*[130]

It also states thus:

> *...provided that the offence has been committed in the name or on the pretext of honour, the imprisonment shall not be less than ten years.*[131]

The amendment has not only increased the penalty in honour crimes cases, but has also limited the right of the legal heir to commute the perpetrator's sentence. Therefore, if there is more than one *wali* and they disagree on the compoundable offence, then the court has the discretion to punish the perpetrator, bearing in mind the facts of the case. Providing space for *wali*(s) to agree on a compoundable offence provides them an opportunity to usurp the victim's right to seek redress. The concept of *wali* also contradicts the principles of gender equality, as in most cases, the *wali* is a man, whose empowerment to decide whether to press charges is based on discrimination.[132]

Although the Criminal Law (Amendment) Act 2004 introduced a few positive changes, it failed to achieve the desired results and fill the obvious lacunae in the law.[133] First, it offered room for the waiver or compounding of perpetrators' sentences, encouraged out-of-court settlements and thus increased

---

[130]ibid; emphasis added.

[131]Pakistani Penal Code, s 311.

[132]Gottesman (n 445).

[133]Aleena Khan, 'Honour Killings in Pakistan: Judicial and Legal Treatment of the Crime: A Feminist Perspective' (2020] 7 LUMS Law Journal 74.

the likelihood of perpetrators being absolved from punishment;[134] and eliminated the provision of redress to victims. Second, the amendment allowed courts to exercise discretion in determining whether to impose a penalty of imprisonment for 10 years in honour crimes cases. The courts may exercise judicial discretion to offer leniency to the perpetrators of honour crimes, who may then evade punishment. The Act does not address the plea of grave and sudden provocation in cases of honour crimes to mitigate the sentence of the accused. Pakistani courts have entertained the plea of grave and sudden provocation as a mitigating circumstance to impose minimal punishments.[135] The definition of honour crimes under Section 299 of the PPC is as follows: 'whether the crime has been committed due to grave and sudden provocation or not'.[136] Therefore, the court is bound to reject the plea of grave and sudden provocation and the accused may be subject to stricter punishments. In honour crimes, social forces, including the Jirga, Panchayat, and the family, play instrumental roles.[137] Social forces play a role in concealing material evidence in honour crimes cases, as a result of which it is difficult to prove the case beyond reasonable doubt.[138] However, the Criminal Law (Amendment) Act neither addresses the threat posed by these deeply ingrained and socially supported institutions nor serves to provide justice and redress to victims. It enables the usurpation of many opportunities for redress.[139]

---

[134]Criminal Law (Amendment) Act 2004 Paragraph 12.

[135]Pope (n 435).

[136]Pakistani Penal Code, s 299.

[137]Amir Zada Asad, 'Honour Killing: A Sociological Analysis' (2004) 31 Journal of Law and Society (University of Peshawar) 1.

[138]ibid.

[139]Qian Hongdao and others, 'Honor Killing Phenomena in Pakistan' (2018) 73 Journal of Law, Policy and Globalization 169.

The Criminal Law (Amendment) (Offences in the Name or Pretext of Honour) Act 2016

In 2016, social media sensation and model, Qandeel Balouch was killed by her brother in the name of honour.[140] Civil society members and women's rights activists staged protests against honour crimes and demanded that changes be made to prevent honour killings and other forms of violence in the name of honour. The Parliament of Pakistan enacted the Criminal Law (Amendment) (Offences in the Name or Pretext of Honour) Act 2016,[141] which amended Sections 290, 302, 309, 310, 338, and 345 of the PPC. It sought to fill the gaps in the legislation to combat honour crimes in the country. It was an important step in the fight against honour crimes in Pakistan.

The Act increased the penalties for honour crimes to 10 years' imprisonment and prescribed the death penalty or life imprisonment in cases of murder committed in the name of honour.[142] The toughening of punishments for honour killings aimed to discourage the crime in the country, as the threat of severe punishments often serves as a deterrent. The most salient and objectionable provisions of the previous law against honour killings were that the legal heir of the victim was entitled to mitigate or remit the punishment of the perpetrator. However, the new law provides that the perpetrator of an honour killing is punishable by death or life imprisonment. The punishment is prescribed by law and cannot be waived or mitigated by the family members of the victim.[143] Making the of-

[140] Sanam Maher, 'Viewpoint: Qandeel Balouch Was Killed for Making Lives Difficult' (*BBC*, 30 September 2019) <www.bbc.com/news/world-asia-49874994> accessed 26 July 2021.

[141] The Criminal Law (Amendment) (Offences in the Name or Pretext of Honour) Act 2016.

[142] ibid.

[143] ibid.

fence non-compoundable by the legal heir is a positive development, as in most honour crimes, the legal heir of the victim is involved in the commission of the crime and can exploit the provision of *qisas* and *diyat* to evade punishment.[144] This Act serves to promote redress for the victim and is an undeniable confirmation that honour crimes are an objective wrong under the laws of Pakistan. However, the imposition of the death penalty on those convicted for committing honour crimes is contested because it is seen as going against the norms of human rights, although it is a legal form of punishment in Pakistan. Like India, Pakistan is 1 of the 56 countries that have retained the death penalty. The tension between international human rights laws that prohibit the death penalty and Pakistani laws that have retained the death penalty can be resolved by pronouncing the death penalty only in rare cases. Similarly, it is essential for the law enforcement agencies to prove the guilt of the perpetrator beyond reasonable doubt and provide the convict access to all legal options including the application to the President of Pakistan for the remission of the death penalty into life imprisonment and/or other lesser punishments.[145] This can decrease the number of death sentences; and with subsequent improvements in the legal system, Pakistan can gradually abolish the death penalty altogether.[146] The Act has extended the scope of *Fasad-fil-arz*,[147] which refers to crimes that cause

[144]Tahir Wasti, 'Islamic Law in Practice: The Application of Qisas and Diyat Law in Pakistan' (2006) 13 Yearbook of Islamic and Middle Eastern Law 97.

[145]Joan Fitzpatrick and Alice Miller, 'International Standards on the Death Penalty: Shifting Discourse' (1993) 19 Brooklyn Journal of International Law 273.

[146]Nazir Ahmad, 'Abolition of Death Penalty: A Case of Pakistan' (2004) 30 Journal of Law and Society (University of Peshawar) 1.

[147]Translated to mean: *Capital Crimes.*

public law and order situations and promote conflict, a significant determinant of the severity of the punishment inflicted on the accused. In this extreme nature of the offence, the threat posed by the offender to the community is taken into consideration. The new law also includes honour crimes under the ambit of *Fasad-fil-arz*.

Some elements of the Criminal Law (Amendment) Act 2016 are subject to criticism.[148] The law states that the prosecution has to prove the motive behind the commission of a crime.[149] If the prosecution is successful in proving that the crime has indeed been committed to protect the honour of a family, only then will the court impose the punishment prescribed for honour crimes. It is most likely that the accused will claim otherwise or deny the motive of honour to avoid the strict punishment prescribed for honour crimes. It is difficult to prove the motive behind the commission of a crime.[150] Similarly, the question of honour may result in the public scrutiny of women's lives and conduct, and may violate their right to privacy, which, in turn, may discourage women from approaching a court of law.[151]

Section 302 of the PPC states that a perpetrator of a simple murder case will be liable to imprisonment for life or the death penalty.[152] The perpetrator of an honour crime may contest the motive of the crime and claim that it was simple murder. This way, the perpetrator can escape the mandatory punishment im-

---

[148]Khan (n 466).

[149]The Criminal Law (Amendment) (Offences in the Name or Pretext of Honour) Act 2016, art 7 (4).

[150]Heydari Arash, Teymoori Ali, and Trappes Rose 'Honor killing as a dark side of modernity: Prevalence, common discourses, and a critical view' (2021) 60 Social Science Information 86.

[151]Chitnis (n 70).

[152]Pakistani Penal Code, s 302.

posed in cases of honour crimes and can be charged under Section 302 of the PPC, instead. In such cases, the family members of the victim may exercise the right to *qisas* and *diyat* and waive the punishment of the accused as these elements are still present in law and apply to offences other than honour crimes. Therefore, the mandatory punishment provided in the Criminal Law (Amendment) Act 2016 may not be very effective. The discretionary power of the judge will eventually decide whether the crime is a murder or an honour killing and that discretionary power may be exploited.

Third, although the Criminal Law (Amendment) Act 2016 addresses honour killings, there are no effective provisions for other kinds of honour crimes that do not amount to murder. Whereas honour killings constitute the most severe form of honour crimes, many other offences are committed in the name of honour, such as forced marriages, harassment, and humiliation.[153],[154] Physical assault and many other types of violence are inflicted upon people in the name of honour. However, these other forms of violence are not adequately addressed in this law. There is no substantial remedy for survivors of honour crimes. Owing to the remaining legal loopholes, the Criminal Law (Amendment) Act 2016 has not achieved the desired results.

Judicial Precedents Pertaining to Honour Crimes in Pakistan

Pakistan's judicial system comprises the Supreme Court, High Courts, and several lower courts. The judicial system has

[153]Roder (n 347).

[154]Chesler (n 11).

played a significant role in addressing honour crimes. Its judgments have been instrumental in the development of the law in Pakistan. Some major judgments addressing honour crimes are discussed below. It is important to analyse these judgments in order to understand the role of the judicial system in dealing with honour crimes. It is also important to understand the problems in the formal justice system that contribute towards the social support for the Jirga and Panchayat systems in Pakistan.

Federation of Pakistan v Gul Hassan and Others

The Zia regime introduced the Hudood Ordinance in 1979[155] and incorporated the *hadd* punishments into the penal laws of Pakistan. *Hudood* refers to offences that are mentioned in the Holy Quran along with prescribed punishments.[156] However, the Zia regime was reluctant to introduce the Islamic punishments of *qisas* and *diyat* into the penal laws of Pakistan. In *Federation of Pakistan v Gul Hassan and Others*,[157] two petitioners approached the Shariat Bench of the Peshawar High Court and challenged the provisions of the PPC pertaining to bodily injury and murder. The petitioners had committed murder, but the victim's family members pardoned them.[158] In Islamic law, *qisas* and *diyat* empower the legal heirs of a victim to forgive and absolve the perpetrator of all legal charges.[159] However, the penal laws of Pakistan did not recognise or incorporate *qisas* and *diyat*. Therefore, the petitioners claimed that the sections of the PPC pertaining to bodily injury and

---

[155]The Hudood Ordinance 1979.

[156]ibid, art 2(c).

[157]*Gul Hassan* (n 440).

[158]ibid.

[159]Palo (n 442).

murder contradicted the principles of Islamic law.[160] The Shariat Bench of the Peshawar High Court reviewed the provisions of the PPC and held that Sections 299 to 338 dealing with murder and bodily injury were repugnant to Islamic injunctions.[161],[162] The court reviewed the provisions of the Code of Criminal Procedure (CRPC) and held that Section 245 of the CRPC[163] also contradicted Islamic injunctions.[164] It held that Islamic injunctions provide for the concept of *qisas* and *diyat* in offences committed against the human body. However, as the provisions of the PPC and CRPC do not mention *qisas* and *diyat*, they do not align with the Islamic concept of justice.[165] To make the laws conform to Islamic injunctions, the Shariat Court directed the incumbent government to incorporate *qisas* and *diyat* into the penal laws of the country. The government challenged this judgment before the Shariat Appellate Bench of the Supreme Court of Pakistan,[166] which upheld the judgment of the Shariat Bench of the Peshawar High Court, and directed the government to incorporate *qisas* and *diyat* into the national penal laws in order to bring them into conformity with Islamic injunctions.[167]

As the Zia regime was reluctant to include qisas and diyat in the penal legislation, it delayed this process. These concepts were finally incorporated into national law in the 1990s. The Shariat Bench ruling in *Federation of Pakistan v Gul Hassan*

---

[160]*Gul Hassan* (n 440).

[161]Pakistani Penal Code, s 299 to s 338.

[162]*Gul Hassan* (n 440).

[163]Criminal Procedure Code, s 245.

[164]*Gul Hassan* (n 440).

[165]ibid.

[166]ibid.

[167]See judgment of the Supreme Court.

and others played a crucial role in the adoption of the *Qisas and Diyat* Ordinance, which changed the criminal justice system.[168] In the past, the state was entitled to prosecute offenders as criminals against the state. However, *Qisas and Diyat* Ordinance gave the victim's family members the option of claiming *qisas* or forgiving the offender, which leads to a miscarriage of justice, especially in honour crimes cases. The family members who committed the crime or any other form of violence in the name of honour have the support of their families, whereas the victim's family members forgive the accused. Therefore, the incorporation of these concepts into the PPC results in the accused avoiding serious charges in most honour crimes, which, in turn, denies the victim's right to redress and does nothing to recognise the objectively wrong nature of honour crimes.

The State v Muhammad Hanif and Five Others

Muhammad Hanif and his two brothers were accused of murdering Muhammad Ashraf.[169] Both brothers denied the charge, but Muhammad Hanif confessed and claimed that it was gravely and suddenly provoked. He claimed that the deceased had dishonoured his wife and he had committed murder under this provocation. He said: 'I myself caused the death of Muhammad Ashraf in a state of grave and sudden provocation when he dishonoured and dragged my wife on the day of the incident'.[170] The trial court accepted the confession and held that:

> *Muhammad Hanif has taken the plea of a grave and sudden provocation which is not available to him now as Section 300 PPC has been substituted by a new Sec-*

[168]Palo (n 442).

[169]*State v Muhammad Hanif and 5 Others* 1992 SCMR 2047.

[170]ibid.

> *tion 300, PPC and the exceptions contained in the old section have been deleted. The definition of Qatl e-i-Amd has been given in the new Section 300, PPC Any-how it serves as a mitigating circumstance in favor of Muhammad Hanif.*[171]

The state legislature amended PPC Section 300, and the plea of aggravated and sudden provocation was removed from the statute. However, the court reinstated the plea of aggravated and sudden provocation for honour crimes to impose a more lenient sentence on the offender and recognised the plea as a relevant factor in imposing more severe sentences.[172] The court clarified that the amendment to Section 300 of the PPC modified the plea of grave and sudden provocation. However, it reintroduced the plea and held that grave and sudden provocation was still relevant in mitigating the defendant's sentence.[173] Muhammad Hanif was sentenced to 10 years' imprisonment and a fine, which he had to pay as compensation (*arsh*) to the family members of the victim. This case is important for another reason. The court held that men are the protectors of women (*qawwam*),[174] and are therefore responsible for protecting their wives. If a person commits an offence against a woman, her male relatives or members of the community have the right to take action against the person for the sake of protection and self-defence. The court's ruling reinforces patriarchal notions of male supremacy, in which women are seen as the property of men that must be protected and are unable to defend themselves because they depend on men for protection.

---

[171]ibid; emphasis added.

[172]ibid.

[173]ibid.

[174]Translated to mean: duty of care [towards women].

Justice Shafi ur Rehman said that the *qisas* is applicable when the victim has not committed any act punishable by death or is not *masoom-ud-dam*.[175] That is, if the victim is accused of a crime punishable by death and is not innocent, then the perpetrator will not be liable for the death penalty or imprisonment for life as provided in the PPC for murder. The concept of *masoom-ud-dam*[176] is exploited in honour cases in order to mitigate the sentence of a perpetrator. If a woman is accused of having a relationship with a man outside marriage, it is considered adultery (*zina*), which is punishable by death in Islam. In such cases, the murder of the victim is justified and the perpetrator can escape legal consequences. The court's ruling in this case resulted in negative consequences for victims of honour killings, especially women. This shows how difficult it is to take a progressive path in Pakistani jurisprudence to better protect the principles of gender equality.

Ali Mohammad v Ali Muhammad

The concepts of *masoom-ud-dam*,[177] sudden provocation, and *qawwam*[178] were discussed in *Ali Mohammad v Ali Muhammad,*[179] where the accused killed a man he had allegedly seen in a compromising position with his wife. The accused took the plea of grave and sudden provocation and the trial court accepted the plea, as provided for in Exception 1 of Section 300 of the PPC, and sentenced the accused to seven years' imprisonment with fine. The judgment was passed after Exception 1

---

[175]*Muhammad Hanif* (n 502).

[176]'under legal protection'.

[177]'under legal protection'.

[178]The Islamic concept of men being in charge of women.

[179]***Ali Mohammad v Ali Muhammad* PLD 1996 SC 274.**

was removed from the law and the plea was not available under the statute.[180] However, the judge wrongly invoked the repealed legal provision and pronounced a judgment under the old PPC provisions, saying that the defence of property/person and honour is a virtuous act and quoted the hadith of Prophet Muhammad (PBUH): 'He who lays down his life while defending his person or property is *shaheed*'. The judge inferred that Islam extends the right to take the life of the aggressor in a given situation to the accused. The judges also recognised the role of men as protectors of women.[181] They referred to Verse 34 of *Sura Al Nisa*, which reads 'Men are in charge of women'.[182] The judges deduced that men, as protectors of women, are entitled to protect women's honour. Thus, if someone attacks a woman's honour, her husband, father, brother, and/or other male family members are entitled to take action to restore the family's honour. Thus, the judgment justified killings in the name of honour. This verdict was challenged before the High Court and then the Supreme Court of Pakistan. The High Court acquitted the accused on appeal and considered the killing lawful. The Supreme Court invoked the concept that men are responsible for protecting women's honour, and accordingly, the right to self-defence includes the right to defend one's wife's honour. The accused was sentenced to two years' imprisonment, but as he had already served the term, he was acquitted.[183]

The defence of grave and sudden provocation has been used by Pakistani courts to offer leniency to the perpetrators of hon-

[180]ibid.

[181]ibid.

[182]Verse 34 of *Sura Al Nisa* of the Holy Quran.

[183]*Ali Mohammad* (n 512).

our crimes.[184] The amendment of Section 300 deleted this defence. However, in this case, the court reinstated the plea and pronounced a judgment based on it, as raised by the defendant. This set a negative precedent for lower courts, which could invoke the same provision to allow a plea that does not exist in the law, in order to justify honour crimes. Perpetrators of honour crimes may invoke this defence to avoid due process of law. The ruling may also have a negative impact on women's status in society, as it recognises men as responsible for women, which makes women more vulnerable. This judgment by the higher courts is contrary to the Constitution of Pakistan, which protects the right to life of every human being.[185] It neither proclaims that honour crimes are grave wrongs nor supports victims right to seek redress.

Ashiq Hussain v Abdul Hameed

Abdul Hameed shot Hafizan Bibi and Abid Hussain, both juvenile victims, when they were working in the cotton fields. The perpetrator claimed severe and sudden provocation, arguing that he had lost his self-control when he saw Hafizan Bibi (his niece) and Abid Hussain in an intimate relationship.[186] The trial court accepted his defence and sentenced him to seven years' imprisonment.[187] However, the verdict was challenged before the Lahore High Court, which allowed the appeal, disregarded the lower court's verdict under Section 302 (b) of the PPC, and

[184]Cheema (n 439).

[185]Constitution of Pakistan, art 9.

[186]*Ashiq Hussain v Abdul Hameed*, 2002, PCRLJ-Lahore High Court, 859.

[187]ibid.

sentenced the accused to death as a *tazeer*.[188] The court enhanced the punishment and imposed a fine, which was payable to the heirs of the victims, and rejected the defence of grave and sudden provocation.[189] It referenced the primary sources of Islamic law and held that Islam protects the rights of men and women.[190] The judge noted that the Holy Quran condemns the cruel and unjust practices that prevailed in the pre-Islamic era, including the killing of children and discrimination against women. The judge discussed the culture of honour killings that prevails in different parts of the country and the need for a legal instrument to prevent such crimes. The court stated:

> *Legislation alone will not eliminate karo kari.[191] Society too has to play its part. Certain social attitudes, especially those that relate to the role and place of women in a community, prevail in large parts of society. This means police officials, especially those from rural backgrounds, or even members of the judiciary, might think that those who commit such murders do no wrong because such actions are allowed by certain tribal or other customs and traditions.[192]*

The judgment reflects the deep-rooted cultural practices that promote such crimes. The court condemned these practices and declared them violations of fundamental rights and proclaimed thus:

---

[188] An Islamic legal concept that means 'punishment for offenses at the discretion of the judge'.

[189] ***Ashiq Hussain* (n 519).**

[190] ibid.

[191] Urdu term for honour killing; emphasis added.

[192] ***Ashiq Hussain* (n 519), para 29.**

> *No court and no civilised human being can sanctify murders in the name of tradition, family honour or religion.*[193]

This is significant because honour killings had been justified in the earlier judgments of higher courts and the perpetrators were justified in their acts of seeking to escape the consequences. In this case, however, the court made it clear that the cultural practices that justify any form of violence against women and customs that justify serious crimes such as murder are blatant violations of the law of the land.[194] The court clarified that honour killings contradict the teachings of Islam and cited several verses from the Holy Quran, to prove that men and women are entitled to equal protection before law. This ruling was a positive precedent for lower courts as it recognised the wrong committed, provided redress and remedies to victims, and promoted the guarantee of fundamental rights based on the principles of gender equality. This case is interesting because the courts relied on religious scriptures to support their decision. It also reflects the influence of religion on the Pakistani legal system. However, the use of religious scriptures by courts is problematic because they are open to multiple interpretations and can be used by different actors to pursue very specific interests. Therefore, the courts must base their judgments on the law rather than on religious scriptures.

Sanobar Khan v The State

The victim went to the baithak (sitting area) to prepare the cot for her son. Her maternal uncle's son came in and they began talking to each other. When the culprit saw them talking, he

---

[193]ibid, para 6.

[194]***Ashiq Hussain*** **(n 519).**

murdered both of them for the sake of family honour. The accused compromised with the family members of the victims and asked the court to release him.[195] However, the court rejected his application and held that the crimes committed in the name of honour were not punishable under the new law against honour crimes and imposed the death penalty on the defendants. This verdict was challenged before the High Court and Supreme Court, both of which affirmed the judgment. The Supreme Court ruled thus:

> *The National Assembly has amended the law to deter and prevent killings in the name or on the pretext of honour killing due to which hundreds of people especially women lost their lives every year. The offence has now been termed to be non-compoundable and it will be covered under the domain 'Fasad-fil-arz' if committed in the name or on the pretext of honour.*[196]

This was a progressive ruling that upheld the amendment to the law and affirmed that perpetrators cannot escape legal consequences by compromising with the legal heir of the victim, as crimes committed in the name of honour are not punishable. This confirms the judiciary's position that honour crimes are objective wrongs whose punishment cannot be evaded. The legal heir of the victim is no longer be entitled to forgive the perpetrators of honour crimes, which is another major step towards guaranteeing reparations to the victim, albeit posthumously. This is an important development that can prevent the miscarriage of justice in honour crimes.

---

[195] ***Sanobar Khan v The State*, PCrLJN-Peshawar-High-Court 181 (2017).**

[196] ibid; emphasis added.

The precedents of higher courts in *Federation of Pakistan v Gul Hassan and Others,*[197] *State v Muhammad Hanif and 5 Others,*[198] and *Ali Mohammad v Ali Muhammad*[199] show that Pakistan's higher courts have reinforced the social norms of the subordination of women. The precedent in the Gul Hassan case led to the inclusion of *qisas and diyat* in the criminal laws of the country, resulting in the miscarriage of justice, especially in cases of honour crimes. In the Muhammad Hanif and Ali Mohammad cases, the court recognised the men as responsible for the women and accepted the male family members' right to self-defence in a case of honour crime. The precedents in both these cases also reaffirmed the concept of *massoom-ud-dam,*[200] which has been used as a means of exploitation. These three and other similar judgments have set negative precedents and have protected archaic and patriarchal social norms. They have also misinterpreted the references from the primary source of Islam to give lenient punishments. However, the decisions in *Ashiq Hussain v Abdul Hameed*[201] and *Sanobar Khan v The State*[202] indicate a positive shift in the judicial system of Pakistan.[203] In both these judgments, the courts declared honour crimes contradictory to both the law and to Islamic values. In the Sanobar Khan case, honour crimes were considered as constituting a non-compoundable offence.[204] These judgments may

[197]*Gul Hassan* (n 440).

[198]*Muhammad Hanif* (n 502).

[199]*Ali Mohammad* (n 512).

[200]i.e. 'under legal protection'.

[201]***Ashiq Hussain* (n 519).**

[202]*Sanobar* (n 528).

[203]Khan (n 466).

[204]*Sanobar* (n 528).

improve social conditions and serve as deterrents in honour crimes cases.

Problems in the Formal Adjudicatory System of Pakistan

The Pakistani legislature has enacted anti-honour crime laws and the judicial system of Pakistan has passed progressive judgments[205],[206],[207] to prevent and address honour crimes. However, to make the system more effective, certain problems in the legislative and judicial systems of Pakistan must be addressed.

Misuse of Discretionary Power by the Courts of Law

Pakistan's higher courts have generally treated perpetrators of honour crimes with leniency.[208],[209] Judges have used the concepts of *masoom-ud-dam*,[210] grave and sudden provocation, and *qawwam*[211] to justify honour crimes and, in some cases, honour killings, which constitute blatant violations of national and international human rights instruments that protect gender

---

[205]Syed Imran Haider, Farhana Khattak, and Muhammad Zubair, 'The Implementation Challenges to Women Protection Laws in Pakistan' (2018) 3 Global Regional Review 253.

[206]ibid.

[207]ibid.

[208]M Hussain, 'Take My Riches, Give Me Justice: A Contextual Analysis of Pakistan's Honour Crimes Legislation' (2006) 29 Harvard Journal of Law & Gender 238.

[209]ibid.

[210]i.e. 'under legal protection'.

[211]i.e. 'duty of care'.

equality and the right to life. *Masoom-ud-dam*[212],[213] refers to the case in which a person is not guilty of an offence punishable by death. A person who has murdered another person who is guilty of such an offence, for example, a married woman or man who has committed adultery, is entitled to lenient punishments in Islamic law. *Qawwam* implies that men are in charge of women, whom they have to protect.[214],[215] Therefore, they have the right to self-defence to protect a woman's honour. These concepts are based on the superiority of men and are rooted in patriarchal customs, which have no legal basis. In some cases, the courts have reintroduced the plea of grave and sudden provocation, which had been removed from the statute books,[216] thus reinforcing these patriarchal norms and contributing to the increase in honour crimes.[217]

The Incorporation of Religious Laws into the Penal Code

The introduction and incorporation of the Hudood and Qisas and Diyat Ordinances into Pakistani penal laws have resulted in negative consequences for women's rights.[218],[219],[220] The Sharia courts set up to enforce these laws have exacerbated the

---

[212]Khan (n 466).

[213]Hongdao and others (n 472).

[214]Sanchita Bhattacharya 'Status of Women in Pakistan' (2014) 51 Journal on Research of Social Policy <http://lcwu.edu.pk/ocd/cfiles/Pakistan%20Studies/Maj/Pak-St-205/statusofwomen.pdf>accessed 26 July 2021.

[215]Khan (n 466).

[216]Cheema (n 439).

[217]Hadi (n 62).

[218]Chakrabarti (n 25).

[219]Cheema (n 439).

[220]Qadeer (n 448).

problems and encouraged various forms of violence. The concepts of *qisas and diyat* were exploited by perpetrators to escape punishment by compromising with the family members of their victims. However, the Criminal Law Act (Amendment) (Offences in the Name or Pretext of Honour) 2016 amended the law and prescribed severe punishments for honour crimes. The Act made honour crimes non-compensable. The sentence imposed by a court cannot be reduced because of the gravity of the crime. The law made honour crimes non-compensable.[221] However, perpetrators of honour crimes may conceal the motive behind their act to avoid severe punishment, and may escape criminal consequences by invoking the concepts of *qisas and diyat*, which are available in cases of murder. Therefore, the amendment of the law may not be very effective in cases of honour crimes.

Disproportionately Low Representation of Women in the Judicial System of Pakistan

The precedents of higher courts in Pakistan show that judges in numerous cases have endorsed patriarchal norms. A more inclusive judiciary with equal representation of men and women may be helpful in bringing about gender sensitivity, as women judges may be more sensitive to the issues faced by women victims; similarly, women victims may feel more comfortable discussing their cases with women judges.[222] Therefore, it is essential to ensure the equal representation of women in the Pakistani legal system to challenge patriarchal norms in the wording of judgments, promote gender sensitivity in the legal

---

[221] non-compoundable offences are the more serious offences in which the parties cannot compromise.

[222] Christina A Madek, 'Killing Dishonor: Effective Eradication of Honor Killing Note' (2005) 29 Suffolk Transnational Law Review 53.

system, facilitate the lives of female honour crime victims, and pursue principles of gender equality. Pakistan has endorsed the CEDAW[223] and the Beijing Declaration and Platform for Action,[224] which states thus:

> *...women have the same rights as men to be judges, advocates or other officers of the court and commit themselves to establish the goal of gender balance in the judiciary.*[225]

However, the representation of women in the judiciary and other law enforcement agencies remains low.[226] Only 7 out of 120 judges in the higher judiciary are women; women are also underrepresented in the lower courts.[227]

Low Reporting and Conviction Rates

Honour killings are considered a private matter in many parts of Pakistan. This results in low reporting rates. Honour killings are reported, but other forms of violence committed in the name of honour are rarely documented. Cases in which victims of honour crimes approach the courts for justice after overcoming all social barriers are usually decided by the courts only after years. The conviction rate for honour crimes is very low, at a mere 2 per cent.[228] There are several reasons for the low

---

[223]Convention on the Elimination of All Forms of Discrimination against Women New York, 18 December 1979.

[224]Beijing Declaration and Platform for Action. The 4th World Conference on Women, 15 September 1995.

[225]ibid, art 232 (m).

[226]Reema Omer, 'Gender Imbalance in Law' *Dawn* (15 March 2016) <www.dawn.com/news/1245694> accessed 26 July 2021.

[227]ibid.

[228]Cheema (n 439).

conviction rate, such as the destruction of evidence and reconciliation between families and witnesses who do not testify in court. Owing to these social structures, most perpetrators of escape the consequences of their crimes. The abuse of discretionary powers given to judges, the involvement of *qisas and diyat*, the disproportionately low representation of women in law enforcement agencies, and the low reporting and conviction rates for honour crimes are some of the major flaws in Pakistan's formal justice system. Other problems, such as outdated investigation methods and deficiencies in the police system, make it difficult to prosecute honour crimes. To promote an effective method of justice, it is important to address these problems.

CHAPTER 4
COMPARISON OF THE FORMAL AND INFORMAL HONOUR CRIME ADJUDICATORY SYSTEMS IN INDIA AND PAKISTAN

Chapters 2 and 3 discussed and analysed the formal and informal judicial systems of India and Pakistan, respectively. This chapter compares the legal instruments and judicial precedents that address honour crimes in both countries. It presents their similarities and differences and the roles they have played in the respective countries. This chapter analyses and compares the informal justice systems of both countries in the form of Panchayat and Jirga and their similarities, differences, and influences. It analyses the systems in both countries to identify common causes for honour crimes, in order to understand the influence of the common historical contexts of India and Pakistan on the development of post-partition legislation, and to determine the approaches adopted in the formal and informal judicial systems of both countries to deal with honour crimes. The comparative analysis can help prescribe measures to address honour crimes in both countries.

Constitutional Provisions

After gaining independence from the British, both countries adopted the Government of India Act 1935[1] to regulate the affairs of the states. Constituent assemblies were created to enact new constitutions for both countries. The Constitution of India came into force in 1950. The first Constitution of Pakistan came into force in 1956, which was then abrogated in 1958. The second Constitution was adopted in 1962, and abrogated in 1969. The present Constitution was enacted in 1973.[2] The Constitutions of both countries reflect the influence of the Constitutions of different democratic countries, particularly the British Common Law principles.[3] Therefore, both have a lot in common. Both Constitutions contain a list of fundamental rights to prevent harmful cultural practices and traditions, including honour crimes. Although the word 'honour crimes' was not explicitly used, the rights listed aim to prohibit certain practices, including honour crimes.[4]

Article 13 of the Constitution of India provides that all laws, customs, rules, regulations, notifications, and traditions shall be in conformity with the fundamental rights guaranteed by it.[5] If a custom, traditional practice, usage, or legal act is incompatible with the fundamental rights enshrined in the Constitution of India, it is void. Article 8 of the Constitution of Pakistan pro-

---

[1]The Government of India Act 1935.

[2]Constitution of Pakistan 1973.

[3]Ronald J Daniels, Michael J Trebilcock, and Lindsey D Carson, 'The Legacy of Empire: The Common Law and Inheritance and Commitments to Legality in Former British Colonies' (2011) 59 American Journal of Comparative Law 111.

[4]Marva Khan, 'Constitutional Comparison and Analysis of Discrimination against Religious Minorities in Pakistan and India' (2014) 1 LUMS Law Journal 19.

[5]Constitution of India, art 13.

vides that customs, traditions, laws, and regulations must conform to the fundamental rights enshrined in the Constitution. All laws, customs, traditions, rules, etc., that are incompatible with fundamental rights are void and have no legal force.[6] Honour killings are ubiquitous in both countries and have been practised for centuries. Therefore, they have their roots in traditions and customs. Articles 13 and 8 are consistent with each other and establish similar principles; they were enacted to prohibit harmful cultural practices, including violence in the name of honour, which deprives individuals of the most basic rights guaranteed by the Constitutions.[7]

Article 14 of the Constitution of India prohibits discrimination based on caste, religion, place of birth, sex, etc., and promotes equality.[8] Article 25 of the Constitution of Pakistan embodies the principle of equality and prohibits discrimination on different grounds.[9] Both constitutions protect the right to life and liberty, freedoms of expression and movement, and numerous other rights.[10] The lists of fundamental rights provided in the Constitutions of India and Pakistan reflect the influence of international human rights instruments, mainly the UDHR[11] and the constitutional protection to human rights in different countries, such as the American Bill of Rights.[12] These lists were included in constitutions to bring the countries' laws in line with international legal principles and universally accepted human values. Although the fundamental rights provided in

---

[6]Constitution of Pakistan 1973, art 8.

[7]Madek (n 555) 17.

[8]Constitution of India 1950, art 14.

[9]Constitution of Pakistan 1973, art 25.

[10]Constitution of Pakistan 1973, arts 8 – 28.

[11]The Universal Declaration of Human Rights 1948.

[12]United States Bill of Rights 1791.

both Constitutions are similar, the nature of the two Constitutions differs. The Constitution of India is secular, whereas that of Pakistan has religious connotations. Article 2 of the Constitution of Pakistan reads, 'Islam shall be the state religion of Pakistan',[13] and Article 2A further provides, 'The principles and provisions set out in the objective resolution reproduced in the Annex are hereby made substantive part of the constitution and shall have effect accordingly'.[14] This reflects a religious basis for the Constitution and affirms that the provisions of the Constitution and all other laws in Pakistan must be consistent with the teachings of Islam and that any law that is inconsistent with Islamic precepts is void. The fundamental rights in the Indian Constitution are supreme, whereas those in the Pakistani Constitution are subordinate to the teachings of Islam and religious reasons can be used to undermine them, as is evident in the later stages of legal development in Pakistan.[15] Article 25 of Constitution of India protects all religions and there is no official state religion in India. The Indian legislature, unlike its Pakistani counterpart, is not obliged to legislate according to specific religious scriptures.[16] India is very different from Pakistan with respect to religious denominations. However, there have been religious tensions in India and the State has been accused of following Hindu nationalism in recent times.[17] The

[13]Constitution of Pakistan 1973, art 2.

[14]Constitution of Pakistan 1973, art 2A.

[15]Matthew J Nelson, *Islamic Law in an Islamic Republic: What Role for Parliament?* [2015] School of Oriental and African Studies <https://eprints.soas.ac.uk/22295/1/Nelson_Islamic%20Law%20in%20an%20Islamic%20Republic.pdf> accessed 26 July 2021.

[16]Rehan Aindri Abeyratne, 'Privileging the Powerful: Religion and Constitutional Law in India' (2018) 13 Asian Journal of Comparative Law 307.

[17]Ananthakrishnan (n 329).

secular and religious natures of India and Pakistan, respectively, have played imperative roles in their legislative developments and approaches adopted in terms of relations between citizens and State institutions.[18]

The Role of Religion in Legislative Developments

In 1976, the central legislature introduced the 42nd Amendment of the Constitution of India to reiterate the secular nature of the State.[19] In *S.R. Bommai v. Union of India,* the Supreme Court of India held that India has been a secular republic from its inception and that the State and religion are separate.[20] Therefore, religion has no place in the law-making process and other matters of the State.[21] However, some approaches adopted by the Indian state are at odds with its secular position. One of these is the legitimacy of personal laws of different religious communities in India, a very diverse country with millions of followers of different religions such as Hinduism, Buddhism, Islam, and Sikhism. The Indian state accepts the personal laws of different religious communities, which means that the followers of a particular religion are subject to their personal

[18]Dian AH Shah, 'The Law and Politics of Religion and Constitutional Practices in Asia Editorial' (2018) 13 Asian Journal of Comparative Law 207.

[19]Forty-Second Amendment of the Constitution of India, 1950.

[20]*S.R. Bommai v Union of India* [1994] AIR 1918; 1994 SCC (3) 1, 11 March.

[21]Gary J Jacobsohn, *The Wheel of Law: India's Secularism in Comparative Constitutional Context* (2nd edn, Princeton University Press 2003).

laws.[22] The legitimacy of personal religious laws has led to controversial issues such as the legality of polygamous marriage, divorce, and inheritance. Personal laws are used to exploit unlawful practices based on discrimination and serve as a justification for perpetrators of honour crimes to avoid the consequences of the crime committed.[23]

India's religious diversity is also reflected in its laws. However, several practices are rooted in the religious beliefs of India's inhabitants that run counter to basic human rights and principles of gender equality. The caste system has its roots in the religious system of Hinduism, which divides people into different categories. It determines a person's social status and duties, role in religious rituals, and job prospects.[24] Dharmendra Kumar Singh[25] described the dynamics of inter-caste marriages and legal relationships in detail. Couples opting for inter-caste marriages are reported to be among the most vulnerable targets of honour crimes in India.[26] Members of one caste consider themselves superior to those of other castes, and marriage to a member of a lower caste is condemned and considered the defilement of the upper caste. People who cross caste boundaries and violate the rules of the caste system – for example, if a member of a higher caste marries a member of a

---

[22]DK Srivastava, 'Personal Laws and Religious Freedom' (1976) 18 Journal of the Indian Law Institute 551.

[23]Bharti Chhibber, 'Women's Rights Are Human Rights' (2018) 22 World Affairs: Journal of International Issues 122.

[24]Manali S Deshpande, *History of the Indian Caste System and Its Impact on India Today* [2010] California Polytechnic <https://digitalcommons.calpoly.edu/socssp/44/> accessed 26 July 2021.

[25]Dharmendra Kumar Singh, 'Inter-Caste or Inter- Religious Marriages and Honour Related Violence in India' (2017) 6 International Journal of Humanities and Social Science Invention 49.

[26]ibid.

lower caste – are considered grave faults.[27] Members of the caste resort to all means, including violence, to maintain their caste boundaries, commit honour crimes against inter-caste couples, and impose various sanctions to ensure compliance with caste boundaries.[28] Chapter 2 showed that the Legislative Assembly did not uphold the caste system and enacted the Hindu Marriage Act[29] to legalise inter-caste marriages. The provisions of this Act protect couples in inter-caste marriages and impose a duty on law enforcement agencies to do the same.[30]

Owing to the secular nature of India, the religion of the majority of the population – Hinduism – did not have a substantial impact on legislative development.[31] The legislature has enacted numerous laws to eliminate harmful cultural practices and reduce the influence of religion. For example, members of the scheduled castes are discriminated against and most honour killings are committed against them. To prevent discrimination and integrate members of the scheduled castes, the Indian legislature enacted the Scheduled Castes and Scheduled Tribes (Prevention of Atrocities) Act, 1989,[32] which prohibits all forms of discrimination against the lower castes and integrates them fully into society. It not only protects their right to life, but also protects them from honour crimes and other discriminatory practices. The legislature has enacted many laws to

---

[27]ibid.

[28]ibid.

[29]Hindu Marriage Act 1955.

[30]ibid.

[31]Jacobsohn (n 582).

[32]Prevention of Atrocities Act (n 231).

promote harmony between religions and legalise interfaith marriages.[33]

Historically, India's central legislature has upheld secular principles and enacted laws to prevent discrimination and protect the human rights of its residents. However, although legal instruments have played an important role in protecting the rights of victims, honour crimes continue to prevail because of the socio-political dynamics of society. Discrimination against members of lower castes remains widespread in India. With the rise of Hindu nationalism, discrimination against religious communities, especially Muslims, is on the rise in India.[34] Hindu nationalist parties are believed to employ different means to create hatred against the members of other religious communities, which may undermine the secular identity of India.[35] Growing Hindu nationalism also creates inter-religious tensions, which may increase the number of honour crimes committed against inter-religious couples.[36]

Religion has influenced legislative developments in Pakistan and was instrumental in the struggle for Pakistan's independence from British rule.[37] The two-nation theory divided the

---

[33]Verma Shweta, Sukhramani Neelam 'Interfaith Marriages and Negotiated Spaces' (2018) 4 Society and Culture in South Asia 16.

[34]Christophe Jaffrelot, (2019), the Fate of Secularism in India, Carnegie Endowment for International Peace <https://carnegieendowment.org/2019/04/04/fate-of-secularism-in-india-pub-78689> accessed 26 July 2021.

[35]Milan Vaishanav, (2019), Religious Nationalism and India's Future, Carnegie Endowment for International Peace <https://carnegieendowment.org/2019/04/04/religious-nationalism-and-india-s-future-pub-78703> accessed 26 July 2021.

[36]Sudha Ramachandran, 'Hindutva Violence in India: Trends and Implications, Counter Terrorist Trends and Analyses' (2020) 12 International Centre for Political Violence and Terrorism Research 15.

[37]Nasir Islam, 'Islam and National Identity: The Case of Pakistan and Bangladesh' (1981) 13 International Journal of Middle East Studies 55.

people of the subcontinent based on their religion.[38] Although the founder of Pakistan wanted to lay down secular foundations for the country, the role of religion in the legal developments increased over time.[39] In Pakistan, religious doctrines were exploited to gain legitimacy, prompting numerous heads of state to amend the law to include religious tenets. For example, the first Constituent Assembly passed the objective resolution[40] in 1949 that has remained part of the three constitutions as a preamble, which declared Pakistan an Islamic Republic and the injunctions of Islam are the yardsticks to determine the legitimacy of laws in Pakistan.[41] Manzooruddin[42] argued that military dictator Ayyub Khan created the Islamic Ideological Council to evaluate whether or not the laws of the State aligned with Islamic laws.[43]

The most prominent changes were made in the Zia regime. Owing to geo-political dynamics and the need to gain popularity in the country, Zia introduced an Islamization policy[44] that introduced many changes in the adjective and substantive laws

[38]PC Mathur, 'Theories of Nation Building in the Indian Sub-Continent: A Political Analysis with Special Reference to Emergence of the State of Bangladesh' (1977) 38 Indian Journal of Political Science 435.

[39]BM Chengappa, 'Pakistan: The Role of Religion in Political Evolution' (2008) 24 Strategic Analysis 2155.

[40]Umair Ahmad, 'The Evolution of the Role of the Objective Resolution in the Constitutional Paradigm of Pakistan - From the Framer Intent to a Tool for Judicial Overreach' (2019) 5 LUMS Law Journal 50.

[41]ibid.

[42]Manzooruddin Ahmed and S.M. Sharif, 'Islamic Aspects of the New Constitution of Pakistan' (1963) 2 Islamic Research Institute 249.

[43]ibid.

[44]Ali Shan Shah, Muhammad Waris, and Abdul Basit, 'Islamization in Pakistan: A Critical Analysis of Zia Regime' (2016) 1 Global Regional Review 260.

of the State.[45] These changes include amendments to the Evidence Act[46] to Qanoon Shahadat,[47] to make it consistent with Islamic injunctions. These changes exacerbated the already prevalent discrimination against women. For example, the testimony of two female witnesses is considered equivalent to that of one male witness in financial matters.[48] The principle of *tazkiyah al shahood*[49] has been exploited in *hadd* cases to defame female witnesses and question the credibility of their testimonies.[50] Similarly, numerous provisions were added to discriminate against women.[51]

The Zia regime also laid the foundation for a parallel legal system in Pakistan by establishing Sharia courts,[52] which were established to ensure strict compliance with Islamic laws in Pakistan. The precedents of the Sharia court may contradict those of common law courts in Pakistan.[53] The Hudood Ordinances[54] (or the 'Zina Ordinance'), which criminalised premarital and extramarital sex as a criminal offence punishable

---

45ibid.

46Qanun-e-Shahadat Order, 1984 (Law of Evidence).

47'Pakistan - The Qanun e Shahadat Order, 1984 (Law of Evidence)' <www.equalitynow.org/pakistan_the_qanun_e_shahadat_order_1984_law_of_evidence> accessed 26 July 2021.

48Qanun-e-Shahadat (n 607), art 17(a).

49Translated to mean 'the pious character of the witness'.

50Qanun-e-Shahadat Order (n 607), art 17(1).

51Kennedy (n 436).

52Shireen Khan Burki, 'The Politics of Misogny: General Zia-ul- Haq's Islamization of Pakistan's Legal System' (2014) 19 Contemporary Justice Review 103.

53Faisal Naqvi, 'The Curious Case of the Shariat Court' *The News* (10 January 2016) <www.thenews.com.pk/print/89285-The-curious-case-of-the-Shariat-Court> accessed 26 July 2021.

54The Hudood Ordinance 1979.

by *hadd*, was one of the most controversial laws to be incorporated into the penal laws of Pakistan by General Zia. Under the ordinance, convicted unmarried men and women were subject to a penalty of 100 lashes, whereas married men and women were subject to the death penalty. The ordinance imposed inhuman punishments and included a highly criticised procedure to prove guilt.[55],[56] There was no difference between rape and consensual sex. Thus, in many cases, the victims of rape were charged with adultery and subjected to harassment, humiliation, and strict punishments instead of being provided justice.[57]

The Zia regime introduced the Qisas and Diyat Ordinance, which was also exploited by the perpetrators of honour crimes to avoid the consequences of their actions.[58] This ordinance had its roots in the Islamic legal system, which provides for retribution or equal treatment. These laws have led to the privatisation of court procedures and the judiciary. Before the introduction of *qisas* and *diyat*, crimes, including honour crimes, were treated as crimes against the state, and therefore, prosecuted by the state. However, with the introduction of these principles, the legal heirs of the victims were empowered to decide on the consequences of the crime committed.[59] In most cases of honour crimes, legal heirs, close relatives, and/or members of the community are involved in the commission of the crime. Therefore, the legal heirs can use these principles to

---

[55]Burki (n 613).

[56]Moeen H Cheema, 'Cases and Controversies: Pregnancy as Proof of Guilt under Pakistan's Hudood Laws' (2006) 32 Brooklyn Journal of International Law 121.

[57]ibid.

[58]Palo (n 442).

[59]ibid.

prevent the perpetrators, who are usually their close allies, from being punished.[60]

The Indian legislature introduced essential measures to prevent harmful religious practices. The smooth democratic transitions in India's history have led to consistent legislative development. In Pakistan, political uncertainty has led to the enactment of contradictory laws. The transition from democracy to military rule and vice versa has led to significant changes in the law. Military and civilian leaders have exploited religion to gain popularity in the country,[61] as is evident from the regime of General Zia-ul-Haq. Therefore, the role of religion has had a greater influence on the legal developments in Pakistan when compared to those in India.

The application of the analytical framework indicates that the legislative developments in Pakistan have been greatly influenced by religion. The Constitution of Pakistan has made it mandatory to make every law align with the injunctions of Islam.[62] Similarly, the Qisas and Diyat Ordinance, the Hudood Ordinance of 1979, and numerous other laws have been taken from religious scriptures. In some cases, the judges of the superior judiciary have referred to qur'anic verses in their judgments.[63] In India, there is no monopoly of any specific religion. Religious factions are in a continuous struggle to consolidate their position; however, the representativeness of many different religions makes it difficult for any one religion to obtain

---

[60]Palo (n 442).

[61]Roder (n 347).

[62]Clark B Lombardi, 'Can Islamizing a Legal System Ever Help Promote Liberal Democracy: A View from Pakistan Islamic Law and Constitutional Liberty' (2009) 7 University of St. Thomas Law Journal 649.

[63]ibid 672.

State support.[64] Therefore, the Indian legislature has been successful in declaring religious principles and laws contradictory to human rights as illegal, which may strengthen the protection of human rights and the prevention of crimes including honour violence in the country. In comparison, the legislature of Pakistan has incorporated religious rules and principles that have been used to exploit victims and allow perpetrators of crimes, including honour violence, to escape the due process of law.[65],[66]

Comparison of the Indian and Pakistani Penal Codes

The main penal laws in force in India and Pakistan were enacted by the British. After Partition, both countries adopted these penal laws and made some amendments over time to suit the needs of their respective citizens. Therefore, the contents of the IPC and PPC are essentially similar. As discussed in Chapter 2, the IPC contains provisions that can be invoked in honour crimes cases, such as Sections 299 and 300, which punish a person convicted of murder with death or life imprisonment.[67] It also prescribes life imprisonment or imprisonment for 10 years for culpable homicide not amounting to murder. Section 307 provides for sentences of up to 10 years' imprisonment and

---

[64] Arachana Parashar, 'Gender Inequality and Religious Personal Laws in India India's Left Behind' (2008) 14 Brown Journal of World Affairs 103.

[65] Qadeer (n 448).

[66] David T Johnson, 'Murder and Punishment in Pakistan' 2010 (2) Pakistan Journal of Criminology 1.

[67] IPC, s 299 to s 300.

a fine for convicts who threaten to kill another person.[68] These provisions are invoked in cases of honour killings or attempts to commit honour killings. Numerous other provisions of the IPC are invoked in cases of honour crimes, as well. A group of persons usually commits the honour crime with common intention. This is often accompanied by a conspiracy to commit the crime. Therefore, Sections 308, 120A-120 B, 107-116, 34, and 35 of the IPC are invoked in cases of honour crimes committed with intent or through a conspiracy.[69] The IPC does not have a dedicated provision addressing the specific aspects of honour crimes. The Indian legislature has not enacted specific legal instruments to address the particular dynamics and factors involved in violence in the name of honour. Thus, perpetrators of honour crimes escape the consequences for the crimes they commit. The loopholes in the laws help them escape punishment and have a negative impact on society in general, as such crimes are not considered serious offences.[70],[71] Therefore, civil society organisations and human rights groups have called for reforms in the country's penal laws and for the adoption of a special legal instrument to prevent and address violence committed in the name of honour in many parts of India.[72]

The PPC has been amended several times. During the Zia regime, Islamic provisions were added to the Penal Code. Over time, the Pakistani legislature has enacted many progressive laws to protect women's rights. The Criminal Law (Amendment) Act 2004 introduced significant amendments to the PPC

---

[68]IPC, s 307.

[69]IPC, ss 308, 120A, 120B, 107-116, 34 and 35.

[70]Malik Amar, 'Honour Killing in Pakistan' [2014] American Journal of Criminal Law (forthcoming).

[71]Sadiq (n 109).

[72]*Shakti Vahini* (n 298).

in relation to honour crimes.[73] The amendment inserted a clause in Section 299 of the PPC to define honour killings. The definition is very broad and includes offences committed on the basis of honour. The insertion of the definition of honour crimes is considered an important development, as it recognises the specificities of honour crimes and provides for a wide range of offences that may constitute such crimes.[74] The amendment also increased the punishment for honour crimes and sought to address the issue of qisas and diyat introduced by the regime. Although the amendment has provided some clarity on such crimes, it has not addressed the issue of combinability of honour crimes. The Criminal Law (Amendment of Offences in the Name or Pretext of Honour) Act 2016 addressed the issues that were overlooked in the 2004 amendment,[75],[76] and increased the punishment for the perpetrators by adding the death penalty; this was done to prevent them from claiming *qisas* or *diyat*, as a result of which the compoundability issue was resolved.[77] The provisions on grave and sudden provocation cannot be invoked in cases of honour crimes, either, and the courts will not take the plea into account to mitigate the sentence of the convicted.[78]

The provisions of IPC and PPC can be invoked in honour crimes. However, the nature of violence in the name of honour requires specific provisions to address various factors involved in these cases. The IPC does not address honour crimes. Therefore, civil society organisations and human rights groups have

---

[73]The Criminal Law (Amendment) Act 2004.

[74]Hussain (n 380).

[75]Hongdao and others (n 472).

[76]Haider and others (n 538).

[77]ibid.

[78]ibid.

been lobbying for the enactment of specific legal instruments to deal with such crimes. The amendments to the PPC have provided some clarity by providing a broad definition of honour crimes. Similarly, the recent amendment reflects an effort on the part of Pakistani lawmakers to address the problems created by the inclusion of *qisas* and *diyat* in the criminal laws, to reduce the influence of religious principles in the law and to prevent perpetrators from escaping the justice system. Thus, the Pakistani legislature has made significant changes to the law. The Indian legislature can also make similar changes to the IPC in order to address honour crimes.

Comparative Analysis of Judicial Precedents

The higher courts of India have played an important role in protecting the victims of honour crimes by imposing punishment on the perpetrators. The formal judicial mechanism has, can, and does recognise transgressions. Most legislative instruments and judicial precedents are in line with the principles of gender quality and have successfully helped the victims of honour crimes. Chapter 2 discussed the precedents relied on by higher courts in different honour crimes cases, which reflect the role of the judiciary in those crimes. In the Manoj-Babli Honour Killing Case,[79] Babli's family killed the victims for violating the rules of the Khap Panchayat, which consider people of the same *gotra* siblings and prohibits marriage between them. The courts held that a marriage within the same *gotra* is lawful and permissible under the laws of India.[80] The constitu-

[79] *Chandrapati* (n 154).

[80] ibid.

tion and other laws of India protect the right of an individual to marry.[81] In this case, the trial court imposed the death penalty on the perpetrator and sentenced the Khap Panchayat leaders to imprisonment for their role in the honour killings. The court upheld the rule of law and declared the institution of Khap Panchayat contradictory to the laws of India.[82] This judgment is a significant development in honour crimes cases, and may decrease the influence of these institutions and their role in honour crimes. Although the imposition of the death penalty is contested by human rights advocates, its imposition on an honour crime convict indicates the severity of the crime and the strictest punishment to be used to prevent similar incidents in the future.

In *Lata Singh v State of U.P. and Another,*[83] the court took into consideration the issue of inter-caste marriages and declared the caste system a curse for the nation,[84] which has resulted in many negative consequences such as caste-based discrimination, the marginalisation and exploitation of people from low-caste backgrounds, and honour crimes committed in the name of protection of caste purity and honour.[85] In this case, the perpetrators took advantage of the due process of law and enlisted the assistance of law enforcement authorities to place obstacles in the path of the petitioner and her in-laws, so that they were falsely accused of abduction and their freedom of movement and other fundamental rights were violated. The court ordered the law enforcement authorities to ensure the en-

---

[81]Constitution of India, art 14.

[82]*Chandrapati* (n 154).

[83]*Lata Singh* (n 158).

[84]ibid.

[85]Bond (n 169).

forcement of the law.[86] Instead of creating hurdles for victims by supporting the perpetrators, the court directed them to protect the rights of the victims. In this case, the judiciary recognised the problems among law enforcement agencies and directed them to.[87]

Honour violence is committed against women, who are accused of bringing dishonour to the family or society, couples, and the victims' families. In *State of U.P. v Krishna Master and Ors*,[88] six individuals were killed in the name of honour. The Supreme Court held that the killings of six persons in the name of honour constituted a grave violation of human rights and sentenced the convicts.[89] Honour crimes are committed by the family members or close allies of a victim on the pretext of protecting familial or community honour.[90] These perpetrators have a different interpretation of the crimes they commit. However, in *Bhagwan Dass v State of Delhi*,[91] the Supreme Court convicted the father of the victim for committing murder to protect the honour of the family.[92] The court held that honour crimes are barbaric, feudal practices that deserve the death penalty.[93] In *Shakti Vahini v Union of India*,[94] the Supreme Court directed the central and state governments to take preventive, punitive, and remedial measures for the elimination of

---

[86]ibid.

[87]ibid.

[88]*Krishna Master* (n 282) 3 August <https://indiankanoon.org/doc/572710/> accessed 26 July 2021.

[89]ibid.

[90]ibid.

[91]*Bhagwan Dass* (n 289) <https://indiankanoon.org/doc/1422914/> accessed 26 July 2021.

[92]ibid, paras 4-5.

[93]ibid, paras 8(i) – 8(v).

[94]*Shakti Vahini* (n 298).

honour crimes in India.[95] The judgment is binding, and the state institutions are bound to act in compliance with it.[96]

Although there are lacunae in the judicial system of India, some judgments have played a positive role in preventing the violation of human rights. The courts have upheld inter-*gotra*,[97] inter-caste,[98] and inter-religious marriages.[99] The judgments have affirmed the right of individuals to bodily autonomy and to make their own decisions. Severe penalties imposed on perpetrators by the higher courts have deterred the commission of crimes and may deter honour killings in the future. While it is contested that the imposition of severe punishments is not always effective in stopping these practices, it is important to address the root causes of the crimes and hold the convicts accountable for their actions.[100] Judicial precedents show that the judiciary is aware of social realities and wants to play a positive role in eliminating stereotypes that contribute towards the commission of various crimes. In several cases, the courts have indicated that the roots of honour crimes lie in the concept of honour, which is prevalent in society.[101] The courts have considered the causes of honour crimes, such as the customs and traditions practised in different parts of the country, which consider women the guardians of the honour of the family and community. A violation of cultural practices is tantamount to a violation of honour and reveals the role of informal institutions in enforcing such practices. Courts have issued instructions to

---

[95]ibid, para 53.

[96]ibid, para 53(h).

[97]Asad (n 470).

[98]ibid.

[99]ibid.

[100]Richard A. Wasserstorm, 'Strict Liability in the Criminal Law, Stanford Law Review' (1960) 12 731.

[101]Clough (n 203).

state authorities to take action against honour crimes. Judicial precedents of the higher courts of India reflect a progressive approach. However, the situation is different in Pakistan. Some of the judicial precedents as discussed in Chapter 3 reveal positive and negative directions.

The plea of grave and sudden provocation was introduced into the penal law by the British to mitigate sentences in certain circumstances. However, after independence, Pakistan's legislature amended the provisions of the PPC to remove the plea of grave and sudden provocation. As seen in *State v Muhammad Hanif and 5 Others*[102] and *Ali Mohammad v Ali Muhammad*, Pakistani courts have accepted the plea of grave and sudden provocation and declared it a mitigating factor in determining the punishment.[103] Thus, this plea has been used by the perpetrators of honour crimes to mitigate the sentences imposed on them. These to judgments are problematic for many reasons. For example, the judges justified the patriarchal values of society by declaring that men are the *qawwam* or protectors of women and their role extends to protecting women's honour. Similarly, the judgments discussed the concept of *masoom-ud-dam*, where the behaviour of the victim is taken into account before imposing punishments on the convicts.[104] Thus, victims of honour crimes are harassed and humiliated, and other derogatory means are used to denigrate their behaviour.

The concepts of *qisas* and *diyat* have been exploited by the perpetrators of honour crimes for decades.[105],[106],[107] They have

---

[102] *Muhammad Hanif* (n 502).

[103] *Ali Mohammad* (n 512).

[104] **ibid.**

[105] Palo (n 442).

[106] Qadeer (n 448).

[107] Haider and others (n 538).

made such crimes a private affair in which the legal heirs of the victim may commute the sentence or pardon the accused, thus restricting the authority of the state to prosecute criminal cases. In *Federation of Pakistan v Gul Hassan and Others* case,[108] it was clear that the Zia regime was reluctant to include the Islamic punishment of *qisas* and *diyat* in the country's penal laws.[109] However, the Shariat Court declared that the PPC provisions governing assault and murder were contrary to the principles of Islamic law, where the legislature incorporated them into the law. Had the Shariat Court not given this ruling, the provisions on *qisas* and *diyat* may not have formed part of the law and would not have been exploited by the perpetrators of honour crimes. Therefore, this judgment set a negative precedent that had negative consequences for victims of honour crimes. The inclusion of *Qisas* and *Diyat* Ordinance was exploited by those who were convicted of honour crimes in order to avoid punishment, whereas victims of rape and sexual assault were accused of adultery.[110],[111] Thus, victims are reluctant to report crimes committed against them.

Federation of Pakistan v Gul Hassan and others, *State v Muhammad Hanif and 5 others*, and *Mohammad Ali v Muhammad Ali* had a negative impact on victims of honour crimes in Pakistan. Following these decisions, the *Qisas* and *Diyat* Ordinance was incorporated into Pakistan's penal laws and the plea of grave and sudden provocation was allowed by the lower courts following the precedents established in these cases. Recent judgments of the higher courts, however, reflect a change in approach. For example, in *Ashiq Hussain v Abdul*

---

[108]*Gul Hassan* (n 440).

[109]Haider and others (n 538).

[110]Palo (n 442).

[111]Constitution of Pakistan, art 9.

Hameed,[112] the accused took the plea of grave and sudden provocation and, although the trial court accepted the plea; the higher court set aside the trial court's judgment, dismissed the plea of grave and sudden provocation,[113] and imposed the death penalty on the convict.[114] The judgment referred to the primary sources of Islam and held that women and men are equal and the crimes committed in the name of honour are against the teachings of Islam.[115] This judgment reflects a progressive interpretation of Islam.[116] In *Sanober Khan v the State,*[117] the court imposed the death penalty on the convict[118] and held that after the amendments to the PPC, the provisions of *qisas* and *diyat* are no longer applicable to crimes committed in the name of honour.[119] Therefore, the legal heirs cannot waive the accused's punishment, and the convict has to face the punishments imposed on him.[120] In both these cases, the Pakistani judges considered various aspects of honour crimes, such as their causes. These judgments are important precedents for lower courts to follow in handling honour crimes. The progressive interpretation of the primary sources of Islam, the imposition of severe punishments on the convicts, and the rejection of the plea of grave and sudden provocation can serve as effective deterrents to honour crimes.

---

[112]*Ashiq Hussain* (n 519).

[113]ibid.

[114]ibid.

[115]ibid.

[116]ibid.

[117]*Sanobar* (n 528).

[118]ibid.

[119]ibid.

[120]ibid.

The comparative analysis of the precedents of the higher courts of India and Pakistan in honour crimes cases shows that both judicial systems have played an important role in addressing the issue by identifying the causes and dimensions of honour crimes and providing guidance to the state institutions and society on the role(s) they should play in addressing the menace. Although some of the judgments of higher courts in Pakistan may have had a negative impact on victims of honour crimes, recent judgments reflect a more progressive approach. Therefore, the judicial system of both countries has great potential in dealing with crimes committed in the name of honour, although there are still some gaps that need to be addressed.

Comparative Analysis of the Informal Adjudicatory Systems

The informal justice systems in India and Pakistan have many similarities and differences. This section compares the informal adjudicatory systems in both countries and their role in honour crimes. As discussed in Chapter 2, there are two types of Panchayat systems in India, namely Panchayati Raj[121] and Khap Panchayat. The former is a legal institution recognised by Indian law for effective administration at the grassroots.[122] Panchayati Raj members are elected representatives from all segments of society.[123] The Khap Panchayat is an informal system that comprises self-appointed leaders of the community who consider themselves the guardians of customs and traditions.[124]

[121]Matthew (n 134).

[122]ibid.

[123]ibid.

[124]Bharadwaj (n 105).

They employ different means to ensure compliance with the customs and traditions to maintain their status quo.[125] The Khap Panchayat protects traditions that contradict Indian and human rights laws, such as the prohibition on inter-caste and inter-*gotra* marriages.[126]

The Jirga operates in the tribal areas of Pakistan,[127] and has its roots in *Pashtunwali*, which refers to the code of conduct followed by the Pakhtun people.[128] Like the institution of Khap Panchayat, the Jirga comprises self-proclaimed local leaders who employ different means to ensure the strict enforcement of the *Pakhtunwali* culture.[129] There is a strict division of roles between the sexes in Pakistani society. Male and female characteristics are strictly assigned to the respective sexes, and a person's role in the household and society is determined by their gender. For example, women are expected to be caring, nurturing, and submissive, whereas men are expected to be brave, courageous, and strong. The portrayal of these characteristics is also reflected in their daily lives. Women are expected to stay within the confines of their homes and take care of others and perform domestic duties, whereas men are expected to protect their families, participate in public life, and show leadership qualities. Men expressed their physical strength on the battlefields in the past. They are the breadwinners of the family and lineage passes down through men.[130] Women are consid-

---

[125]ibid.

[126]Singh (n 586).

[127]Roder (n 347).

[128]Arab Naz and others, 'The Relational Analyses of Pakhtun Social Organization (Pakhtunwali) and Women's Islamic Rights Relegation in Malakand Division, KPK Pakistan' (2012) 4 International Journal of Sociology and Anthropology 63.

[129]Mahmood and others (n 111).

[130]Roder (n 347).

ered symbols of honour,[131] and the traditions impose different rules of conduct to be observed by women to protect the honour of both the family and tribe.[132] This code of conduct comprises rules that regulate dress codes, behaviours in public, etc.[133] Men are obliged to uphold honour by making sure that women observe the customs. The Panchayat system prevalent in the Sindh and Punjab areas follows similar patterns. The Jirga and Panchayat are based on patriarchal norms.[134],[135] The customs and traditions established by these institutions uphold male supremacy. As Ismail noted, both institutions consider women the symbol of honour and have established a code of conduct that governs their behaviour.[136] These rules and regulations restrict women's freedom, force them to live in a state of constant fear and oppression, and make women subservient to their male counterparts, who have the power to watch over their honour and regulate their behaviour.[137] These institutions deprive women of their basic human rights as guaranteed by the laws of India and Pakistan. They treat women as property, consider them non-existent, and believe that they must be protected and guarded by the male members of society.[138]

The traditions and customs promoted and protected by the institutions of Jirga and Panchayat are based on discrimination against women. Therefore, women are not represented in these

---

[131]ibid.

[132]ibid.

[133]*Lata Singh* (n 158).

[134]Christ (n 44).

[135]Hadi (n 62).

[136]Ismail (n 13).

[137]ibid.

[138]ibid.

institutions,[139] even in cases that concern them. They are not given the opportunity to appear before the institutions and present their truths. Instead, men make decisions on their behalf. These institutions do not consider women human beings, which is evident in their treatment of and attitude towards women. They seek to restrict women's freedom and impose their codes of conduct to control women. The use of force against women, including honour crimes, is a corrective measure justified by these institutions.[140],[141],[142]

The *modus operandi* followed by the Khap Panchayat and Jirga are similar.[143] When a problem or dispute arises in a community, tribe, or caste, or an individual violates the designated code of conduct, the elders gather in one place,[144] and operate as self-proclaimed leaders constituting an assembly that has enormous power.[145] The assembly takes into consideration the facts of the case. In most cases, the parties are not given the opportunity to appear before the assembly and justify[146] or deny the claims made against them.[147] Parties belonging to vulnerable groups[148] such as women and individuals from lower caste or tribal backgrounds have no opportunity to be heard. The assembly pronounces judgments based on their

---

[139]Roder (n 347).

[140]Arab Naz and others (n 690); Mahmood and others (n 114).

[141]Sadiq (n 109).

[142]Ismail (n 13).

[143]Roder (n 347).

[144]ibid.

[145]ibid.

[146]ibid.

[147]D'Lima (n 15).

[148]ibid.

discretion.[149] The procedures followed by the Jirga and Panchayat are not codified[150] but have been formed based on centuries-old practices, which over time.[151] Although there may be some differences in the procedure, the main aspects are similar.[152]

The Khap Panchayat and the Jirga mainly comprise powerful members of society such as feudal lords and/or religious leaders.[153] They use these systems to pursue their own political and economic interests.[154] In most cases, these institutions impose strict sanctions to uphold their authority.[155] Although they do not have an executive body to enforce their judgments, their decisions can be implemented because they enjoy public support and social pressure,[156] which includes isolating a person or the family of the respective persons, imposing economic sanctions, and social boycott.[157] Another similar aspect of the two institutions is the communal system. Both institutions function in societies where the values of the community are highly regarded and the rights of the individual are not taken into account or given the importance they deserve.[158] In the Jirga, be-

---

[149]ibid.

[150]Bharadwaj (n 105).

[151]ibid.

[152]ibid.

[153]Robert Hayden, 'A note on caste panchayats and government courts in India' (1984) 16 Journal of Legal Pluralism and Unofficial Law 43.

[154]Vasudha Nagaraj, 'Local and Customary Forums: Adapting and Innovating Rules of Formal Law' (2010) 17 Indian Journal of Gender Studies 429.

[155]Craig Johnson, Priya Deshingkar, and Daniel Stuart, 'Grounding the State: Devolution and Development in India's Panchayats' (2005) 41 Journal of Development Studies 937.

[156]Sadiq (n 109).

[157]ibid.

[158]ibid.

cause tribal identity is considered most important,[159] tribes go the extra mile to protect their social status.[160] In the Khap Panchayat, the association with a particular caste or community is imperative for their existence.[161]

Although there are many similarities between the Khap Panchayat and Jirga, they operate in different contexts and have different codes of conduct.[162] The Khap Panchayat protects the caste system and maintain caste hierarchy.[163] It protects and enforces traditions such as prohibiting inter-caste and intra-*gotra* marriages.[164] The Panchayat in Punjab and Sindh protects social classes. The Jirga protects tribal values[165] particularly, the code of conduct or the *Pashtunwali.*[166] Caste and tribal systems empower community leaders to make decisions for and exercise power in their communities. Therefore, they use various means, including violence, to enforce the traditions and customs and maintain their status quo.[167] They decide on a range of cases. For instance, the gang rape of Mukhtaran Mai was adjudged by the local Panchayat,[168] the atrocities committed in the Kohistan cases were subject to the diktat of the Jirga,[169] and the brutal murders in the Manoj-Babli case were committed on the orders of the Panchayat.[170]

---

159 ibid.

160 Mahmood and others (n 111).

161 Asad (n 470).

162 Baloch (n 346).

163 ibid.

164 ibid.

165 ibid.

166 *Lata Singh* (n 158).

167 ibid.

168 Farmer (n 377).

169 *Umar Khan* (n 366).

170 *Chandrapati* (n 154).

Both institutions share many similarities.[171] The Jirga and Khap Panchayat have evolved over centuries and exert great influence in society. These institutions operate in patriarchal and patrilineal societies where lineage passes through males who have control over most resources.[172,173] These institutions protect male dominance by safeguarding practices and customs based on discrimination against women.[174] They employ similar means to control women including honour violence to restrict their freedom and maintain the supremacy of men.[175] They impose sanctions and employ the use of force to maintain their authority and enjoy social support[176] for their judgments. However, they differ in terms of their objectives, standard practices, and other aspects. These institutions are illegal,[177] unconstitutional,[178] and unlawful,[179] but play an important role in honour crimes.

---

[171]Baloch (n 346).

[172]ibid.

[173]Chakrabarti (n 25).

[174]Sadiq (n 109).

[175]Kaushal (n 47).

[176]Sadiq (n 109).

[177]***Ashiq Hussain* (n 519).**

[178]*Sanobar* (n 528).

[179]***Ashiq Hussain* (n 519).**

CONCLUSION

This study has three aims. First, it sought to contribute to the literature on honour crimes committed in South Asia, particularly India and Pakistan. Both countries have reported some of the highest numbers of honour crimes[1],[2] and share the same historical context.[3] This study critically analysed the concept of honour in both countries and examined the factors that contribute to violence in the name of honour. The first chapter examined the history of the subcontinent, analysed the different civilisations, and described how the region evolved from a matriarchal society during the Indus Valley Civilisation to a patriarchal one. The advent of foreign invaders from different parts of the world and their settlement in the region contributed to this shift,[4] and resulted in the commission of different forms of violence, including honour crimes against women.[5] The chap-

---

[1]Honour Based Violence Awareness Network: Human Rights Country Report of 2018 <http://hbv-awareness.com/statistics-data/#India> accessed 26 July 2021.

[2]Honour Based Violence Awareness Network: Human Rights Country Report of 2018 <http://hbv-awareness.com/statistics-data/#Pakistan> accessed 26 July 2021.

[3]D'Lima (n 15).

[4]Anjum (n 33).

[5]Chesler (n 11).

ter also analysed the concept of honour[6],[7] and the different dynamics of honour crimes.

Second, reference was made to the two types of systems that exist in India and Pakistan for the adjudication of honour crimes: the formal and informal adjudication systems, which comprise legal instruments enacted by the legislatures of both countries and the precedents established by the Supreme Court and the High Courts in honour crime cases, and the decisions passed by the Khap Panchayat in India and the Jirga and Panchayat in Pakistan, respectively. These organisations are set up by self-appointed community leaders to ensure strict adherence to customs and traditions.[8],[9] This study analysed these two streams of jurisprudence to understand how the problems in the formal system strengthened the Khap Panchayat and Jirga. To better understand the relationship between these informal and formal institutions, this study analysed the relevant legal instruments and judicial precedents of both countries. It also analysed the Jirga and the Panchayat, their historical development, and modus operandi to understand their role in honour crimes.

Building on a comparison of the two systems of justice, this study establishes that the informal institutions contradict human rights and condone honour crimes to maintain their authority. As informal justice systems are rooted in the customs and traditions of their respective societies, they employ various means, including honour crimes, to ensure strict adherence to customs and traditions that run counter to human rights norms. The formal system is criticised for imposing the death penalty.

---

[6]Laham (n 341).

[7]Rodriguez (n 6).

[8]Godara (n 182).

[9]Robina (n 359).

Thus, in comparison, both systems are different because one promotes crisis whereas the other imposes retributive punishment as a preventive measure against such crimes.[10] Cases were also discussed in which the judgments of the Jirga and the Panchayat resulted in serious human rights violations. In numerous cases, both systems have incited and pressured families and community members to commit various crimes in the name of honour. The study also highlights the gaps in the formal legal system that have contributed to the social support of the informal legal system. Based on this, it sought to recommend measures to address these gaps and problems in the formal legal system and reduce social support for the Jirga and Panchayat.

Reflecting on the Concept of Honour Violence

The first part of the study looked at the concept of honour crimes and enumerated the definitions of the crime as formulated by HRW, UNICEF, and other human rights organisations and concluded that honour crimes are acts of violence committed against individuals, mainly women, to protect the honour of the family. Honour is a social construct[11],[12] that refers to an individual or family's social status or reputation in their community or society.[13] The community or society sets a certain standard of behaviour to maintain its social status and prestige. Failure to comply with the standard code of conduct may de-

[10]Asad (n 470).

[11]Laham (n 341).

[12]Rodriguez (n 6).

[13]Robina (n 359).

prive a person or family of the respect or prestige that was previously accorded to them.[14] To regain their lost status, they use violent means against the person accused of violating the standard code of conduct and dishonouring the family. This results in honour crimes. The standard code of conduct in these societies is determined by various factors such as religion, culture, and socio-political dynamics.[15] Therefore, the practices vary from one area to another in both India and Pakistan.[16] Common practices reported to be an important factor in honour crimes include inter-caste, inter-religious, and intra-*gotra* marriages, not following a particular dress code or engaging in practices considered inappropriate in rural India and Pakistan. The standard code of conduct prescribed by these societies is rooted in patriarchy,[17] which protects male dominance. Thus, the standard code of conduct has been designed to maintain traditional gender norms. In these societies, women are considered a repository of honour[18] and have to abide by the roles and codes of conduct that are assigned to and imposed on them, respectively.[19] Men are considered protectors of honour and use various means to control women's behaviour. Honour crimes include various forms of violence such as murder, attempted murder, kidnapping, abduction, torture, forced suicide, acid attack, burning, forced marriage, sexual assault, harassment,

---

[14]ibid.

[15]Roder (n 347).

[16]D'Lima (n 15).

[17]Chakrabarti (n 25).

[18]Kaushal (n 47).

[19]Ismail (n 13).

and gang rape, among others to control women's behaviour and protect the honour of the family.[20,21,22]

Reflecting on the Formal and Informal Adjudicatory Systems

The formal judicial systems in India and Pakistan operate based on laws passed by the Parliament and relevant judicial precedents. The legislatures of both countries have enacted numerous legal instruments to protect and realise universally recognised human rights as enshrined in international human rights instruments. These instruments protect the right of life, freedom of expression, liberty, etc., and seek to prevent practices such as honour crimes. India has no specific legal instrument to address honour crimes. However, many legal instruments can be invoked in cases of honour crimes to punish perpetrators. The relevant legal instruments include Articles 13, 14, 15, 21, and 25 of the Constitution of India, which deal with the illegality of traditions, customs, and laws incompatible with fundamental rights, equality before the law, non-discrimination on the grounds of religion, race, caste, sex, place of birth, etc., security of life and liberty or freedom of religion. These articles of the supreme law of India are relevant in cases of honour crimes that deprive a person of the fundamental rights guaranteed by these constitutional provisions. Similarly, the central legislature of India has enacted numerous laws relevant in cases of honour crimes. These include the Hindu Marriage Act of 1955, which legalises and protects inter-caste couples, one of

[20]Roder (n 347).

[21]Chesler (n 11).

[22]Ismail (n 13).

the most vulnerable target groups for honour crimes. The provisions of the Scheduled Castes and Scheduled Tribes (Prevention of Atrocities) Act 1989, the Protection of Human Rights (Amendment) Act 2006, and the Protection of Women from Domestic Violence Act 2005 prevent customs and traditions that conflict with human rights; therefore, they are invoked in cases of honour crimes to provide justice to victims.[23] The most significant penal legislation in India, the IPC, contains numerous provisions against honour crimes.[24] Sections 299, 300, and 302 are the most important sections of the IPC in dealing with honour crimes, particularly honour killings. These provisions deal with cases of murder and manslaughter and provide for death penalty or life imprisonment for the convicts. Therefore, in cases of honour killing, the courts must impose the death penalty or life imprisonment on the perpetrators under these provisions. Numerous other provisions can also be used to punish the convicts. These legal instruments have protected the people of India and oblige the law enforcement agencies to ensure the implementation of the laws and prevent honour crimes. Similarly, they provide for penalties in case of violations. These penalties can act as a deterrent to prevent such crimes and provide justice to the victims.

The evolution of legislation in Pakistan differs from that in India because of military interventions and the transition from military rule to democratic government throughout Pakistan's history. Religious factors have influenced the evolution of both legislation and judicial precedents. These inconsistencies have led to many problems with legal instruments that have had negative consequences for victims and protected perpetrators of honour crimes. However, over time, the Pakistani legislature

[23]Haider and others (n 538).

[24]Pakistani Penal Code 1860.

has amended many provisions of the law to protect people against honour crimes. Numerous legal instruments are relevant in cases of honour crimes and protect the life and liberty of persons. The most important laws are Articles 8, 9, 15, and 25 of the Constitution of Pakistan. They refer to the illegality of customs, laws, and traditions that are incompatible with fundamental rights, security of life and liberty, freedom of movement and equality before the law respectively. These articles can be invoked to protect the rights of victims, as honour crimes deprive a person of these constitutionally protected rights. Most honour crimes are committed by close allies of victims, including family, relatives, and community members.[25] The Qisas and Diyat Ordinance[26] provided an opportunity for legal heirs to waive the perpetrators' punishment. As the perpetrators committed offences with the support of the victims' legal heirs, they misused the due process of law to avoid the consequences of their actions. Owing to the criticism of this ordinance[27],[28],[29] and the high number of honour crime cases reported in the country,[30] the legislature of Pakistan amended numerous provisions of the PPC. The Criminal Law (Amendment Act) 2004, by inserting a new clause in Section 299, defines honour crimes as offences committed in the name or under the pretext of honour, that is, in the name or under the pretext of

---

[25]D'Lima (n 15).

[26]Qisas and Diyat Ordinance 1990.

[27]Gottesman (n 445).

[28]Constitution of Pakistan, art 9.

[29]National Commission for Human Rights, 'A Study on Honour Killings in Pakistan and Recommendatory Checks through Law' [2019] The Office of the Chairman, National Commission for Human Rights, Government of Pakistan <https://nchr.gov.pk/wp-content/uploads/2019/01/Final-Report-Honour-Killing.pdf> accessed 26 July 2021.

[30]Human Rights Commission of Pakistan (n 361).

karo kari, siyah kari, or similar customs or practices. This definition is very broad and covers all forms of violence committed in the name of honour. The amendments also increase the penalties for cases of honour crimes.

The recent amendment to the PPC titled Criminal Law (Amendment) (Offences in the Name or Pretext of Honour) Act 2016 addresses the problems created by *Qisas* and *Diyat* Ordinance, makes honour crimes non-comprisable and relieves the legal heirs of victims of honour crimes from waiving the sentence or settling out-of-court with the convict. These amendments are considered significant developments[31] that have the potential to play an effective role in curtailing honour crime cases by closing the loopholes that perpetrators use to evade punishment, thus reaffirming that honour crimes are objective wrongs and assuring victims' rights to redress and remedy.

The legislative instruments enacted by India and Pakistan protect honour crime victims and provide a mechanism for the redress of grievances. The judicial precedents in both India and Pakistan show that the judicial system has played an instrumental role in the evolution of laws within these countries and in preventing honour crimes. The decisions in the Manoj-Babli Honour Killing Case,[32] *Lata Singh v the State of U.P. and Another*,[33] *the State of U.P. v Krishna Master and Ors*,[34] *Bhagwan Dass v the State of Delhi*,[35] and *Shakti Vahini v Union of India*[36] in India have reinforced inter-caste, inter-religious, intra-*gotra* marriages, with the courts imposing very strict penalties

---

[31] Haider and others (n 538).

[32] *Chandrapati* (n 154).

[33] *Lata Singh* (n 158).

[34] *Krishna Master* (n 282).

[35] *Bhagwan Dass* (n 289).

[36] *Shakti Vahini* (n 298).

to prevent similar violations of rights. The courts have also provided directives to state institutions to take measures to prevent honour violence and interpret the law in favour of victims. The judgments of the higher courts of Pakistan have protected the rights of victims by imposing serious penalties such as the death penalty or life imprisonment on the convicts of honour crimes. *Ashiq Hussain v Abdul Hameed*[37] set a significant precedent by quoting the primary sources of Islam to provc that honour crimes have no place in the injunctions of the religion and are blatant violations of human rights.[38] In *Sanobar Khan v The State*,[39] the court dismissed the out-of-court settlement and prescribed the death penalty for honour killings. The recent judgments imposing heavy penalties, rejecting the plea of grave and sudden provocation, declaring that honour violence oppose the religious teachings of Islam, and rejecting out-of-court settlements in honour killings cases may prove effective for the prevention of such crimes in Pakistan.

The formal justice systems have played an important role in addressing honour crimes and have shown great potential in dealing with such crimes. However, they have not been able to achieve the desired results in eliminating the social support associated with the informal system. These lacunae are related to the disproportionate representation of women in the judiciary and other law enforcement agencies, which have resulted in misogynistic rulings against the victims of honour violence, as evidenced by some of the precedents of Pakistani courts that have admitted the plea of grave and sudden provocation, the concepts of *masoom-ud-dam* and *qawwam*,[40] to justify the ac-

---

[37]***Ashiq Hussain* (n 519).**

[38]ibid.

[39]*Sanobar* (n 528).

[40]*Ali Mohammad* (n 512).

tions of the perpetrators of honour crimes. Other issues include the influence of religious laws within the penal laws, such as the concept of *qisas* and *diyat* in Pakistani laws and the legitimacy of personal laws in India, which may be exploited by the accused to escape punishment.[41] There are many other obstacles, such as the delay in the pronouncement of judgments in courts, the low reporting and conviction rates, and social acceptance and support of informal adjudication mechanisms and judgments.[42,43]

Despite the issues in the formal systems, the analysis of the institutions of the Jirga and Panchayat establishes that the formal system is the better option. The Mukhtaran Mai[44] and Kohistan cases[45] in Pakistan exposed the role of the Jirga in the promotion of honour crimes. Similarly, Manoj-Babli[46] and numerous other cases indicate that the Khap Panchayat advocates cruel practices and promotes grave violations of human rights in India. These institutions have been using force and means such as isolation, economic sanctions, and social pressure to promote honour violence.[47,48] Therefore, these institutions have been declared unlawful in these countries by their respective apex courts.[49,50]

---

[41]Haider and others (n 538).

[42]Dimri (n 269).

[43]Sadiq (n 109).

[44]Lahore High Court (n 374).

[45]*Umar Khan* (n 366).

[46]*Chandrapati* (n 154).

[47]Singh (n 586).

[48]Sadiq (n 109).

[49]***Ashiq Hussain* (n 519).**

[50]*Sanobar* (n 528).

Recommendations

Despite its problems, the formal court system plays an important role in addressing honour crimes. The precedents have declared the Khap Panchayats and Jirga incompatible with the Constitution and other legal instruments of India and Pakistan, and have effectively made them illegal. Courts have imposed harsh punishments on those convicted of honour crimes to serve as a deterrent and prevent similar crimes in the future. Legislators have invoked instruments to protect the rights of victims and punish those convicted of honour crimes. The Panchayat and Jirga have supported honour crimes by putting pressure on family members to commit them. Therefore, measures should be taken to address the problems in the formal legal system. The study recommends that India and Pakistan must take substantial measures to increase women's representation in the judiciary and other law enforcement agencies, as their presence would increase representation and empathy towards women victims, as they tend to feel more comfortable with women. This can counter the patriarchal mindset prevalent in these institutions, which is reflected in their judgments. Similarly, the inclusion of women in law enforcement agencies can empower them to challenge the patriarchal norms that confine women to the private sphere. This can improve the status of women in their respective countries, and victims of honour crimes will be able to approach law enforcement agencies and the judiciary more confidently and safely to voice their grievances.

Second, justice delayed is justice denied. The judicial systems of India and Pakistan take years to adjudicate civil cases, and decades to adjudicate criminal cases. Citizens do not have confidence in these institutions and turn to the Jirga and Panchayat instead. It is important to ensure speedy adjudication to counter social support for the informal court system. Countries can set up special courts or tribunals to decide and deal with the specifics of honour crimes.

Third, honour crimes have their roots in the patriarchal culture of India and Pakistan. To eradicate the menace of honour killings, it is important to tackle the root of the problem. The government, civil society organisations, and other actors can play important roles in countering the patriarchal culture. It is important to both ensure adequate representation of women in all spheres of life and women's empowerment. It is essential to educate women about their legal rights and give them the confidence to approach the relevant state authorities to resolve their problems.

Fourth, honour crimes are unique and involve a range of factors. Therefore, general penal legislation may not be sufficient to tackle such crimes, as is evident from the recent amendment to the Pakistani Penal Code, which provides a specific definition of honour crimes. Similarly, the Indian legislature should enact special legislation or add provisions to the IPC to address honour crimes. Civil society and human rights organisations in India have also been lobbying for specific laws to address this issue. It is also important to address the negative impacts of religious laws and prevent their influence on criminal law, as shown by the negative consequences of the inclusion of qisas and diyat in Pakistan's criminal law.

Finally, this study found that the Jirga and Panchayat contribute to honour crimes. These institutions perpetuate cultural practices that contradict human rights norms and pressure victims' family members to commit honour crimes in order to ensure strict adherence to traditions and customs and maintain their status quo. Though the Supreme Courts of both India and Pakistan have declared these institutions illegal, they continue to exert great influence. It is therefore recommended that substantive measures be taken to create awareness on the problems caused by these institutions and to increase people's trust in formal state institutions.

BIBLIOGRAPHY

Treaties, Statutes, and Laws

American Legislation

United States Bill of Rights 1791.

Indian Legislation

The Age of Consent Act 1891.
The Bengal Sati Regulation 1829.
The Constitution of India 1950.
The Female Infanticide Prevention Act 1870.
Forty-Second Amendment of the Constitution of India 1950.
The Government of India Act 1935.
The Hindu Widows' Remarriage Act 1856.
The Hindu Marriage Act 1955.
The Indian Penal Code 1860.
The Indian Majority Act 1875.
The Protection of Women from Domestic Violence Act 2005.
The Protection of Human Rights Act 1993 (with Amendment Act 2006).
The Protection of Human Rights (Amendment) Act 2019.
The Scheduled Castes and Scheduled Tribes (Prevention of Atrocities) Act 1989.

The Special Marriage Act 1954.

International Legal Instruments

Beijing Declaration and Platform for Action - the 4th World Conference on Women 1995.
Convention on the Elimination of All Forms of Discrimination against Women 1979.
The Convention against Torture, and Other Cruel, Inhuman or Degrading Treatment or Universal
Declaration of Human Rights 1948, Article 1.
International Covenant on Civil and Political Rights 1966.
International Covenant on Economic, Social and Cultural Rights 1966.
Punishment (CAT) 1984.

Pakistani Legislation

The Alternate Dispute Resolution Act 2017.
The Constitution of the Islamic Republic of Pakistan 1979.
The Criminal Law (Amendment) (Offences in the Name or Pretext of Honour) Act 2016.
The First Constitution of Pakistan 1956.
The Hudood (Zina) Ordinance 1979.
The Pakistan Penal Code 1860.
Qanun-e-Shahadat Order 1984 (Law of Evidence).
Qisas and Diyat Ordinance 1990.
The Second Constitution of Pakistan 1957.

United Kingdom Legislation

The Criminal Law Amendment Act 2004.

Cases

Ali Mohammad v Ali Muhammad PLD [1996] SC 274.

Arumugam Servai v State of Tamil Nadu [2011].

Asha Ranjan v State of Bihar and Ors [2016].

Ashiq Hussain v Abdul Hameed [2002] PCRLJ-Lahore High Court, 859.

Bai Kashi v Jamnadas Mansukh [1912].

Bhagwan Dass v State of Delhi [2011].

Emperor v Dinbandhu Ooriya AIR [1930] Cal 199.

Federation of Pakistan v Gul Hassan and Others PLD [1989] SC 633.

K.M Nanavati v State of Maharashtra AIR [1962] SC (605).

Lahore High Court Multan Bench Multan (Judicial Department) Criminal Appeal No 60 [2002].

Lata Singh v State of U.P. and Another [2006].

Mukhtasir & 5 Others v The State and Bin Yamin [2014] PCr-LJN Peshawar High Court.

Saleh Muhammad v The State PLD [1965] SC 366.

Sanjay v State of Haryana, Crl. in the High Court of Punjab and Haryana at Chandigarh Appeal No. 662- DB [2005].

Sanobar Khan v State, 2018 PCrLJN Peshawar High Court 181 [2017].

Shakti Vahini v Union of India [2018].

Smt. Chandrapati v State of Haryana and Others [2011] (Manoj-Babli).

S.R. Bommai v Union of India [1994] AIR 1918, SCC (3) 1.

State of U.P. v Krishna Master Ors AIR [2010] SC 3071.

State v Mohammad Umar Khan, Saeer and Sabir [2012] PCR 9376.

State v Muhammad Hanif and 5 Others [1992] SCMR 2047.

State v Vikas Yadav Vishal Yadav, S.C. No. 78 [2002].

Books

A. L. (ed.), *Society and the sexes in medieval Islam* (Malibu, California: Undena 1979), 63-68.

Ahmad N, *Women in Islam* (APH Publishers 2011).

Ahuja R, *Indian social system* (Rawat Publications 2006).

Ahuja R, *Social problems in India* (Rawat Publications 2006).

Ali R, *The dark side of 'honour': Women victims in Pakistan* (Arqam 2001).

Arendt H, *On violence* (Harvest Books 1970).

Auboyer J, *Daily life in ancient India: From 200 BC to 700 AD* (Phoenix Press 2002).

Bhasin K and Menon R, *Borders & boundaries: Women in India's partition* (1st edn, Kali 1998).

Briggs J (trs), *The rise of the Mahomedan power in India: Power in India till the year A. D. 1612* (Originally written by Muhammad Kasim Ferishta, Tarikh-i Firishta, Vol. II, Arthur Probsthain 1829).

Chakravarti U, *Gendering caste: Through a feminist lens* (Stree 2003).

Chaturvedi RG, *Manusmriti* (Universal Publications 2010).

Chaudhary P, *Contentious marriages, eloping couples, gender, caste and patriarchy in Northern India* (Oxford University Press 2007).

Coole D, *Women in political theory: From ancient misogyny to contemporary feminism* (Lynne Rienner Publishers 1993).

Coward H, *Human rights and world's major religions: The Hindu tradition* (Praeger Publisher 2005).

Deutsch KA, *Muslim women in colonial north India circa 1920-1947: Politics, law and community identity* (1st edn, Cambridge 1998).

Devi I, *Social stratification setup and new approaches to sociology* (Institute for Sustainable Development and Anmol Publication 1998).

Dewan VK, *Law relating to offences against women* (Orient Law House 2000).

Dhagamwar V, *Law, power and justice* (Sage Publications 1992).

Dobash RE and Dobash RP, *Rethinking violence against women* (Sage Publications 1998).

Dowson J, *The history of India, as told by its own historians: The Muhammadan period*, vol 1 (Edited from the Posthumous Papers of the late Sir H M Elliot, Trubner Paternoster Row 1867).

Dube L, *Women and kinship: Comparative perspectives on gender in South and South East Asia* (United Nations University Press 1997).

Dutta PK, *Craving blocs: Communal ideology in twentieth century Bengal* (Oxford University Press 1999).

Fanon F, *The wretched of the earth* (Penguin Modern Classic 1961).

Fateh NF, *Honour killing* (1st edn, University of Toronto 2012).

Gernard R, *Violence and the scared* (A & C Black 1972).

Goodwin J, *The price of honour: Muslim women, lift the veil of silence on the Islamic world* (Warner Books 1995).

Hassan Y, *Heaven become hell: A study of domestic violence in Pakistan* (Shirkat Ghat Special Bulletin 1995).

Jacobsohn GJ, *The wheel of law: India's secularism in comparative constitutional context* (2nd edn, Princeton University Press 2003).

Jodhka SS and Naudet J, *Mapping the elite: Power, privilege, and inequality* (1st edn OUP 2019).

Johnson AG, *Patriarchy, the system, gender knot* (Temple University Press 1997).

Khan MH, *Pardah and polygamy: A study in the social pathology of Muslim society* (Nashiran-e-Ilm-o-Taraqiyet 1972).

Khan TS, *Chained to customs* (The Review 1999).

Khan TS, *Beyond honour* (Oxford University Press 2006).

Lerner G, *The creation of patriarchy* (Oxford University Press 1986).

Liddle J and Joshi R, *Daughters of independence: Gender, caste, and class in India* (Kali for Women & Zed Books 1986).

Mandelbaum GD, *Women's seclusion and men's honor: Sex roles in north India, Bangladesh and Pakistan* (The University of Arizona Press 1988).

Marshall J, *Mohenjo-Daro and the Indus Valley civilisation* (2nd edn, Probsthain 1931).

Marx K and Engels F, *Collected works* (Lawrence & Wishart 1976).

Matthew G, *Status of Panchayati Raj in the states and union territories of India, 2000* (Concept Publishing Company 2000).

Mayell H, *Thousands of women killed for family honour* (National Geographic News 2002).

Mayer AE, *Islam and human rights: Tradition and politics* (3rd edn, Westview Press 1999).

Meeto V and Mirza HS, *Honour, violence, women and Islam* (Routledge 2011).

Mernissi F, *Beyond the veil: Male-female dynamics in modern Muslim society* (Indiana University Press 1987).

Mishra A. (2012). *Honour killings: The law it is and the law it ought to be.* Manupatra. Retrieved from Manuputra.com/articles.

Mohanty M, *Class, caste, gender* (1st edn, Sage Publications 2004).

Mojab S and Abdo N, *Violence in the name of honour: Theoretical and political challenges* (Bilgi University Press 2004).

Murgai SR, *Women in South and South East Asia* (1st edn, University of Tennessee 2004).

Nanda, BR, *Indian women: From Purdah to modernity* (1st edn, Advent Books Division 1990).

Omvedt G, *Violence against women: New movements and new theories in India* (Kali for Women 1990).

Podsetnik V and Spirkin A, *A glance at historical materialism* (Progress Publishers 1965).

Pope N, *Honour killings in the twenty first century* (1st edn, Palgrave Macmillan 2012).

Rana SA, *Women in India social and cultural History* (ABC Clio 2009).

Roder TJ, *Non-state justice institutions and the law* (1st edn, Springer 2015).

Saadwai NE, *The hidden face of Eve: Women in the Arab world* (ZED Press 1980).

Sharma KL, *Indian social structure and change* (Rawat Publications 2007).

Shrivastava N, *The progress of Indian women from 1900s to present* (1st edn, University of Connecticut 2009).

Welchman L and Hossain S, *Honour* (Zed Books 2005).

Journal Articles and Book Chapters

Abeyratne RA, 'Privileging the Powerful: Religion and Constitutional Law in India' (2018) 13 Asian Journal of Comparative Law 307.

Abu-Lughod L, 'Seductions of the "Honor Crime" (2011) 22 Differences: A Journal of Feminist Cultural Studies 17.

Abu-Odeh L, 'Comparatively Speaking: The "Honor" of the "East" and the "Passion" of the "West"' (1997) Utah Law Review 287.

Abu-Odeh L, 'Honor: Crimes of' in S Joseph (ed), *Encyclopedia of Women and Islamic Cultures* (Brill 2005).

Agha N, 'Kinship in rural Pakistan: Consanguineous marriages and their implications for women' (2016) 54 Women's Studies International Forum 1.

Ahmad N, 'Abolition of Death Penalty: A Case of Pakistan' (2004) 30 Journal of Law and Society (University of Peshawar) 1.

Ahmad U, 'The Evolution of the Role of the Objective Resolution in the Constitutional Paradigm of Pakistan- From the Framer Intent to a Tool for Judicial Overreach' (2019) 5 LUMS Law Journal 50.

Ahmed M and Sharif SM, 'Islamic Aspects of the New Constitution of Pakistan' (1963) 2 Islamic Research Institute 249.

Ali SS, 'Is an Adult Muslim Woman *Sui Juris*? Some Reflections on the Concept of "Consent in Marriage" without a *Wali* (with particular reference to the Samia Waheed case)' (1996) 3 Yearbook of Islamic & Middle Eastern Law 30.

Amar M, 'Honour Killing in Pakistan' American Journal of Criminal Law (March 19, 2014). Forthcoming.

Ambasta K, 'An Unclear Empiricism: A Review of the Death Penalty India Report' (2017) 13 Socio-Legal Review 130.

Anjana R, 'Mask of Honor-Causes behind Honor Killings in Pakistan' (2006) 12 Asian Journal of Women's Studies 88.

Anjum T, 'The Emergence of Muslim Rule in India: Some Historical Disconnects and Missing Links' (2007) 46 Islamic Studies 217.

An-Na'im A, 'State Responsibility under International Human Rights Law to Change Religious and Customary Laws' in RJ Cook (ed) *Human Rights of Women: National and International Perspectives* (University of Pennsylvania Press 1993).

An-Na'im A, 'The role of "community discourse" in combating 'crimes of honour': preliminary assessment and prospects' in L Welchman and S Hossain (eds) *'Honour': Crimes, paradigms and violence against women* (Zed Books 2005).

Arash H, Ali T, and Rose T, 'Honor killing as a dark side of modernity: Prevalence, common discourses, and a critical view' (2021) 60 Social Science Information 86.

Asad AZ, 'Honour Killing: A Sociological Analysis' (2004) 31 Journal of Law and Society 1.

Asamoah Y, 'Women's Human Rights and "Honor Killings" in Islamic Cultures' (1999/2000) 8 Buffalo Women's Law Journal 21.

Bagchi J, 'Female Sexuality and Community in Jyotirmoyee Devi's Epar Ganga Opar Gonga' in M Thapan (ed) *Embodiment: Essays on Gender and Identity* (Oxford University Press 1997).

Baker NV, Gregware PR, and Cassidy MA, 'Family Killing Fields: Honour Rationales in the Murder of Women', (1999) 5 Violence Against Women 164.

Bangash MA, 'Administrative Justice in the Tribal Areas' (1997) XVIII Journal of Law & Society 39.

Bannerji H, 'Age of Consent and Hegemonic Social Reform' in C Midley (ed) *Gender and Imperialism* (Manchester University Press 1998).

Barakatullah A and Imran AS, 'Jirga System in Pakhtun Society: An Informal Mechanism for Dispute Resolution' (2013) 5 Pakistan Journal of Criminology 45.

Baxi P, Rai SM, and Ali SS, 'Legacies of Common Law: "Crimes of Honour" in India and Pakistan' (2006) 27 Third World Quarterly 1239.

Beckett AMC and Macey M, 'Race, gender and sexuality: The oppression of multiculture' (2001) 24 Women Studies International Forum 309.

Bharadwaj SB, 'Myth and Reality of the Khap Panchayats: A Historical Analysis of the Panchayat and Khap Panchayat' [2012] 28 Studies in History 43.

Bhatia M, 'Domestic Violence in India: Cases Under the Protection of Women from Domestic Violence Act, 2005' (2012) 32 South Asia Research 103.

Bhattacharya S, 'Status of Women in Pakistan' (2014) 51 Journal on Research of Social Policy

Bond J, 'Honor as Property' (2012) 23 Columbia Journal of Gender and Law 202.

Bureau L, 'Analysis on honour killing' (2021) 10 Lawz Media 10.

Burki SK, 'The Politics of Misogyny: General Zia-ul- Haq's Islamization of Pakistan's Legal System' (2014) 191) Contemporary Justice Review 103.

Butalia U, 'Abducted and Widowed Women: Questions of Sexuality and Citizenship During Partition' in M Thapan (ed) *Embodiment: Essays on Gender and Identity* (Oxford University Press 1997).

Chakrabarti S, 'Interpreting the Legacy of Partition in the Subcontinent: Indian and Pakistani Perspectives' (2016) 40 Politeja 21.

Chakravarti U, 'Conceptualizing Brahmanical Patriarchy in Early India: Gender, Caste, Class and State' (1993) 28 Economic and Political Weekly 579.

Chakravarti U, 'From fathers to husbands: of love, death and marriage in North India', in L Welchman and S Hossain (eds), *'Honour': Crimes, paradigms and violence against women* (Zed Books 2005).

Cheema MH, 'Cases and Controversies: Pregnancy as Proof of Guilt under Pakistan's Hudood Laws' (2006) 32 Brooklyn Journal of International Law 121.

Cheema MH, 'Judicial Patronage of Honour Killings in Pakistan: The Supreme Court's Persistent Adherence to the Doctrine of Grave and Sudden Provocation' (2008) 14 Buffalo Human Rights Law Review 22.

Cheema SA, 'Non-Repugnancy Decisions of the Federal Shariat Court of Pakistan: An Analysis of Politico- Legal Ramifications' (2020) 7 LUMS Law Journal 48.

Chengappa BM, 'Pakistan: The Role of Religion in Political Evolution' (2008) 24 Strategic Analysis 2155.

Chesler P and Bloom N, 'Hindu vs. Muslim Honor Killings' (2012) 19 Middle East Quarterly 43.

Chhibber B, 'Women's Rights Are Human Rights' (2018) 22 World Affairs: The Journal of International Issues 122.

Chitnis V, 'The Legacy of Colonialism and Women Rights in India' (2007) 64 Washington Lee Law Review 1315.

Chowdhury P, 'Enforcing Cultural Codes, Gender and Violence in Northern India', in K Jayawardena and M de Alwis (eds) *Embodied Violence, Communalising Women's Sexuality in South Asia* (Kali for Women 1996).

Christ CP, 'A New Definition of Patriarchy: Control of Women's Sexuality, Private Property, and War' (2016) 24 Feminist Theology 214.

Clough A, 'Honour Killings, Partial Defences and the Exclusionary Conduct Model' (2016) 80 Journal of Criminal Law 177.

Connors J, 'United Nations approaches to "crimes of honour"' in L Welchman and S Hossain (eds), *'Honour': Crimes, paradigms and violence against women* (Zed Books 2005).

Coomaraswamy R and Kois L, 'Violence Against Women' in KD Askin and DM Koening (eds) *Women and International Human Rights Law* (Transnational Publishers 1999).

Coomaraswamy R, 'Identity Within: Cultural Relativism, Minority Rights and the Empowerment of Women' (2002) George Washington International Law Review 1.

Coulson N, 'Regulation of Sexual Behaviour under Traditional Islamic Law' in Al-Sayyid-Marsot.

Csanad A, 'Legal Transplantation in India Colloquium' (2009) 2009 Jura: A Pecsi Tudomanyegyetem Allam- es Jogtudomanyi Karanak tudomanyos lapja 185.

D'Lima T, Solotaroff JL, and Pande RP, 'For the Sake of Family and Tradition: Honour Killings in India and Pakistan' (2020) 5 Indian Journal of Women and Social Change 22.

Daniels RJ, Trebilcock MJ, and Carson LD, 'The Legacy of Empire: The Common Law and Inheritance and Commitments to Legality in Former British Colonies' (2011) 59 American Journal of Comparative Law 111.

Das V, 'National Honour and Practical Kinship: Of Unwanted Women and Children' in *Critical Events: An Anthropological Perspective on Contemporary India* (Oxford University Press 1995).

Deol SS, 'Honour Killing in India: A study of the Punjab state' (2014) 3 International Research Journal of Humanities and Social Sciences 7.

Derné S, 'Hindu Men Talk about Controlling Women: Cultural Ideas as a Tool of the Powerful' (1994) 37 Sociological Perspectives 203.

Dhull K, 'Honor Killing in India' (2017) 2 International Journal of Advanced Educational Research 417.

Dubey AK, 'Honour Killing: The Socio-Legal Perspective and Judicial Approach' (2017) 17 International Journal of Research in Social Sciences 101.

Elakkary S and others, 'Honour Crimes: Review and Proposed Definitions' (2014) 10 *Forensic Science, Medicine and Pathology*, 76.

Fane H, 'The Female Element in Indian Culture' (1975) 34 Asian Folklore Studies 51.

Fitzpatrick J and Miller A, 'International Standards on the Death Penalty: Shifting Discourse' (1993) 19 Brooklyn Journal of International Law 273.

Galanter M, 'Snakes and Ladders: Suo Moto Intervention and the Indian Judiciary Symposium: Layers of Law and Social Order' (2014) 10 FIU Law Review 69.

Galtung J, 'Cultural violence', (1990) 27 Journal of Peace Research 291.

Galtung J, 'Violence, peace and peace research', (1969) 6 Journal of Peace Research 167.

Geetha V, 'On Bodily Love and Hurt' in M John and J Nair (eds), *A Question of Silence? The Sexual Economies of Modern India* (Kali For Women 1998).

Gottesman E, 'The Reemergence of Qisas and Diyat in Pakistan' (1992) 23 Columbia Human Rights Law Review 433.

Gupta K, 'Gender Based Violence: Honour Killings' (2014) 8 Asian Journal of Development Matters 178.

Gupta M, 'Strengthening the Backward Class: Role of National Commission for Backward Classes' (2018) 8 GNLU Journal of Law Development and Politics 93.

Hadi A, 'Patriarchy and Gender Based Violence in Pakistan' (2017) 10 European Journal of Social Sciences, 297.

Haeri S, 'The Politics of Dishonour: Rape and Power in Pakistan' in M Afkhami, *Faith and Freedom: Women's Human Rights in the Muslim World* (I.B. Tauris 1995).

Haider SI, Khattak F, and Zubair M, 'The Implementation Challenges to Women Protection Laws in Pakistan' (2018) 3 Global Regional Review 253.

Hassan R, 'Feminism in Islam' in S Young and K Young (eds) *Feminism and World Religions* (State University of New York Press 1999).

Hayden R, 'A note on caste panchayats and government courts in India' (1984) 16 Journal of Legal Pluralism and Unofficial Law 43.

Hongdao Q and others, 'Honour Killing Phenomena in Pakistan' (2018) 73 Journal of Law, Policy and Globalization 169.

Hussain M, '"Take My Riches, Give me Justice:" A Contextual Analysis of Pakistan's Honor Crimes Legislation' (2006) 29 Harvard Journal of Law & Gender 223.

Hussain N, 'The Narrative Appropriation of Saima: Coercion and Consent in Muslim Pakistan' in N Hussain, S Mumtaz, and R Saigol (eds) *Engendering the Nation-State* (Simorgh Women's Research and Publication Centre 1997).

Hussain N, 'Women as objects and women as subjects within fundamentalist discourse' in NS Khan, R Saigol and AS Zia (eds) *Locating the Self: Perspectives on Women and Multiple Identities* (ASR Publications 1994).

Hussain R, 'Islamization: An Analysis of Religious, Political and Social Change in Pakistan' (1985) 21 Middle Eastern Studies 263.

Husseini R, 'A comparative study of the reform work conducted in Asia and Europe to combat violence and 'so-called' honour murders' in MM Idriss and T Abbas (eds) *Honour, Violence, Women and Islam* (Routledge 2011).

Idriss MM, 'Honour, violence, women and Islam – an introduction' in MM Idriss and T Abbas (eds) *Honour, Violence, Women and Islam* (Routledge 2011).

Ishaq HH, 'The Right to Fair Trial: Better Late than Never' (2014) 1 LUMS Law Journal 96.

Islam N, 'Islam and National Identity: The Case of Pakistan and Bangladesh' (1981) 13 International Journal of Middle East Studies 55.

Ismail Z, 'The Communal Violence Bill: Women's Bodies as Repositories of Communal Honour' (2020) 21 Journal of International Women's Studies 50.

Jan G and Munir K, 'Honour Killings: A Socio-Legal Analysis with Special Reference to District Srinagar of J&K' (2018) 2 Sociology International Journal 335.

Jillani TH, 'Implementing the Right to Marry – A View from the Pakistan Courts' (2001) International Family Law 25.

Jodhka SS and Shah G, 'Comparative Contexts of Discrimination: Caste and Untouchability in South Asia' (2010) 45 Economic and Political Weekly 99.

Johnson C, Deshingkar P, and Stuart D, 'Grounding the State: Devolution and Development in India's Panchayats' (2005) 41 Journal of Development Studies 937.

Johnson DT, 'Murder and Punishment in Pakistan' 2010 (2) Pakistan Journal of Criminology 1.

Johnson PS and Johnson JA, 'The oppression of women in India, violence against women', (2001) 7 Sage Publication.

Kachhwaha K, 'Khap Adjudication in India: Honouring the Culture with Crimes' (2011) 6 International Journal of Criminal Justice Sciences 297.

Karanjawala T and Chugh S, 'The Legal Battle against Domestic Violence in India: Evolution and Analysis' (2009) 23 International Journal of Law, Policy and the Family 289.

Kashyap D, 'Death Penalty in India' (2013) Asian Journal of Legal Studies 70.

Katiyar A and Sri N, 'Honor Killing - A Social Evil in Modern Indian Society' (2020) 2 International Journal of Juridical Studies & Research 8.

Kaushal K, 'No Honour in Honour Killing: Comparative Analysis of Indian Traditional Social Structure vis-à-vis Gender Violence' (2020) 5 ANTYAJAA: Indian Journal of Women and Social Change 52.

Kelly JM, 'Audi Alteram Partem' (1964) Natural Law Forum 103.

Kennedy CH, 'Islamization and Legal Reforms in Pakistan, 1979-1989' (1990) 63 Pacific Affairs 62.

Khan A, 'Honour Killings in Pakistan: Judicial and Legal Treatment of the Crime: A Feminist Perspective' (2020) 7 LUMS Law Journal 74.

Khan M, 'Constitutional Comparison and Analysis of Discrimination against Religious Minorities in Pakistan and India' (2014) 1 LUMS Law Journal 19.

Kumar A, 'Public Policy Imperatives for Curbing Honour Killing in India' (2012) 1 Politics & Governance 33.

Kumar N, 'Judicial Response Towards Khap Panchayat' (2013) 2 Journal of Global Research and Analysis 108.

Laham SM and others, 'Emotional and Behavioural Reactions to Moral Transgressions: Cross-Cultural and Individual Variations in India and Britain' (2010) 45 International Journal of Psychology 64.

Leader-Elliott I, 'Passion and insurrection in the law of sexual provocation' in N Naffisen and RJ Owens, *Sexing the Subject of the Law* (Sweet and Maxwell 1997).

Lehr-Lehnardt R, 'Treat Your Women Well: Comparisons and Lessons from an Imperfect Example across the

Waters' (2002) Southern Illinois University Law Journal 403.

Leonard K and Weller S, 'Declining Subcaste Endogamy in India: The Hyderabad Kayasths, 1900-75' (1980) 7 American Ethnologist 504.

Liddle J and Joshi R, 'Gender and Imperialism in British India' (1985) 5 South Asia Research 147.

Lombardi CB, 'Can Islamizing a Legal System Ever Help Promote Liberal Democracy: A View from Pakistan Islamic Law and Constitutional Liberty' (2009) 7 University of St. Thomas Law Journal 649.

Luopajarvi K, 'International Accountability for Honour Killings as Human Rights Violations' (2004) 22 Nordisk Tidsskrift for Menneskerettigheter 2.

MacKinnon CA, 'Sex Equality under the Constitution of India: Problems, Prospects and Personal Laws' (2006) 4 International Journal of Constitutional Law 181.

Madek CA, 'Killing Dishonor: Effective Eradication of Honor Killing Note' (2005) 29 Suffolk Transnational Law Review 53.

Mahmood A, Ullah S, and Ashfaq S, 'The Evolution of Jirga System: A Conflict Resolution Mechanism in FATA' (2018) 2 Liberal Arts and Social Sciences International Journal 21.

Mahmud J, 'Crimes against Honour: Women in International Refugee Law' (1996) 9 Journal of Refugee Studies.

Manan A, 'Child Marriage in South Asia and its Dialectic Relationship with Law and Society' (1997) XVIII Journal of Law and Society 79.

Mathur PC, 'Theories of Nation Building in the Indian Sub-Continent: A Political Analysis with Special Reference to Emergence of the State of Bangladesh' (1977) 38 Indian Journal of Political Science 435.

Menon R and Bhasin K, 'Abducted Women, the State and Questions of Honour' in K Jayawardena and M de Alwis (eds) *Embodied Violence, Communalising Women's Sexuality in South Asia* (Kali for Women 1996).

Modi I, 'Society and Sociology in India: Some Reflections' (2012) 178 Polish Sociological Review 141.

Moghadam M, 'Patriarchy and the politics of gender in modernising societies: Iran, Pakistan and Afghanistan' (1992) International Sociology 35.

Moody P, 'Love and law: Love Marriage in Delhi' (2002) 36 Modern Asian Studies.

Moore EP, 'Honor: South Asia' in S Joseph (ed) *Encyclopedia of Women and Islamic Cultures* (Brill 2005).

Moxnes H, 'Honor and Shame' in RL Rohrbaugh (ed) *The Social Sciences and New Testament Interpretation* (Hendrickson 1996).

Murugananthan S, 'Honour Killings: The Menace - A Case Study in Tamil Nadu' (2014) 1 International Journal of Management Research and Social Science.

Nagaraj, 'Local and Customary Forums: Adapting and Innovating Rules of Formal Law' (2010) 17 Indian Journal of Gender Studies 429.

Naqvi T and Korai KM, 'Yakta-e-Rozgar', in S Wistro (ed), *Karo-kari* (Weer Publication 2000).

Narasimhan G, 'Revisiting S.105 of the Indian Evidence Act, 1872' (1998) 10 Student Advocate 52.

Naz A and others, 'The Relational Analyses of Pakhtun Social Organization (Pakhtunwali) and Women's Islamic Rights Relegation in Malakand Division, KPK Pakistan' (2012) 4 International Journal of Sociology and Anthropology 63.

Noor S, 'Karo Kari: a curse and a crime' in S Wistro (ed), *Karo Kari. Karachi* (Weer Publication 2000).

Palmer M, 'The People's Republic of China: Problems of Marriage and Divorce' 1988-89 27 Journal of Family Law 57.

Palo S, 'A Charade of Change: Qisas and Diyat Ordinance allows Honor Killings to go Unpunished in Pakistan' (2008) 15 UC Davis Journal of International Law and Policy 93.

Panhwar U and others, 'Critical Analysis of the Impact of Job on the Social Status of Women in Pakistan' (2017) 8 Journal of Education and Practice 17.

Parashar A, 'Gender Inequality and Religious Personal Laws in India India's Left Behind' (2008) 14 Brown Journal of World Affairs 103.

Patil S, 'Some Aspects of Matriarchy in Ancient India: Clan Mother to Tribal Mothers' (1973) 2 Social Scientist 42.

Rai R, 'Inter-Caste Marriages and Reservation Policy in India: A Socio-Legal Study' (2016) 1 International Research Journal of Social Science & Humanities 56.

Ramachandran S, 'Hindutva Violence in India: Trends and Implications, Counter Terrorist Trends and Analyses (2020) 12 International Centre for Political Violence and Terrorism Research 15.

Ramseshan G, 'The construction of honour in India criminal Law: An Indian Lawyer perspective, honour, violence, women and Islam' in MM Idrrissad and T Abbas (eds) *<Book Title>* (Routledge 2011).

Rana PK and Mishra BP, 'Honour Killing: A gross violation of human rights its challenges' (2013) 2 International Journal of Humanities and Social Inventions 24.

Rankin GC, 'The Personal Law in British India' (1941) 89 Journal of the Royal Society of Arts 426.

Raza A, 'Mask of Honor-Causes behind Honor Killings in Pakistan' (2006) 12(2) Asian Journal of Women's Studies 88.

Relis T, 'Unifying benefits of studies in legal pluralism: accessing actors' voices on human rights and legal pluralities in gender violence cases in India' (2016) 48 Journal of Legal Pluralism and Unofficial Law 354.

Robina AN, 'Jirga and Panchayat as the Precursor to Honour Killing in Pakistan' (2020) <www.qurtuba.edu.pk/thedialogue/The%20Dialogue/15_1/15_1_12.pdf> accessed 26 July 2021.

Rodriguez PM, 'The Role of Honour Concerns in Emotional Reaction to Offences' (2002) 16 Cognition and Emotion 143.

Roover JD, 'Scheduled Castes vs. Caste Hindus: About a Colonial Distinction and Its Legal Impact' (2017) 13 Socio-Legal Review 22.

Rout N, 'Role of Women in Ancient India' (2016) Odisha Review 42.

Sen P, 'Crimes of honour', value and meaning' in L Welchman and S Hossain (eds), *'Honour': Crimes, paradigms and violence against women* (Zed Books 2005).

Sen S, 'Offences Against Marriage' in ME John and J Nair (eds) *A Question of Silence? The Sexual Economies of Modern India* (Kali For Women 1998).

Shah AS, Waris M, and Basit A, 'Islamization in Pakistan: A Critical Analysis of Zia Regime' (2016) 1 Global Regional Review 260.

Shah DAH, 'The Law and Politics of Religion and Constitutional Practices in Asia Editorial' (2018) 13 Asian Journal of Comparative Law 207.

Shah N, 'Faislo -- The Informal Settlement System' in Shirkat Gah (ed) *Shaping Women's Lives: Laws, Practices and Strategies in Pakistan* (Shirkat Gah 1998).

Shah N, 'Role of the Community in Honour Killings in Sindh' in N Hussain, S Mumtaz, and R Saigol (eds) *Engendering the Nation-State* (Simorgh Publications 1998).

Shaheed F, 'Engagements of Culture, Customs and Law: Women's Lives and Activism' in Shirkat Gah (ed) *Shaping Women's Lives: Laws, Practices and Strategies in Pakistan* (Shirkat Gah 1998).

Shaheed F, 'The Experience in Pakistan' in M Davis (ed) *Women and Violence* (Zed Books 1994).

Siddiqui DM, 'Of consent and contradiction: forced marriages in Bangladesh' in L Welchman and S Hossain (eds), *'Honour': Crimes, paradigms and violence against women* (Zed Books 2005).

Singh A, 'Honour Crime and Khap Involvement: Threat to Human Rights' (2014) 24 Deliberative Research 28.

Singh AK, 'Paradox between Universalism of Human Rights and Relativism of Culture: A Case Study of Honour Killings in India' (2020) 4 Journal of Southeast Asian Human Rights 253.

Singh AK, 'The Meandering Course of Death Penalty Sentencing in India: A Critical Analysis' (2015) 5 Nirma University Law Journal 19.

Singh D and Bhandari DS, 'Legacy of Honor and Violence: An Analysis of Factors Responsible for Honor Killings in Afghanistan, Canada, India, and Pakistan as Discussed in Selected Documentaries on Real Cases' (2021) 11 SAGE Open 21582440211022З.

Singh DK, 'Inter-Caste or Inter-Religious Marriages and Honour Related Violence in India' (2017) 6 International Journal of Humanities and Social Science Invention 49.

Singh G, 'Honour-Related Violence against Women in India: Problems, Perspectives and Challenges' (2016) 5 Journal of Social Work and Development Issues 80.

Singh V, 'Khap Panchayats: Honor Killings in India' (2015) <www.researchgate.net/publication/297346507_Khap_-

Panchayats_Honor_Killings_in_India> accessed 26 July 2021.

Srivastava DK, 'Personal Laws and Religious Freedom' (1976) 18 Journal of the Indian Law Institute 551.

Steiker CS, 'No, Capital Punishment Is Not Morally Required: Deterrence, Deontology and the Death Penalty' (2005) 58 Stanford Law Review 751.

Talukdar R and Chaudhury M, 'The Special Marriage Act 1954' (2020) 57 Psychology and Education 1007.

Tamara R, 'Unifying benefits of studies in legal pluralism: accessing actors' voices on human rights and legal pluralities in gender violence cases in India' (2016) 48 Journal of Legal Pluralism and Unofficial Law 354.

Thomas DQ and Levi RS, 'Violence Against Women: An Introduction' in KD Askin and DM Koening (eds), *Women and International Human Rights Law* (Transnational Publishers 1997).

Verma S and Sukhramani N, 'Interfaith Marriages and Negotiated Spaces' (2018) 4 Society and Culture in South Asia 16.

Viswanath K, 'Shame and Control: Sexuality and Power in Feminist Discourse in India', in M Thapan (ed), *Embodiment: Essays on Gender and Identity* (Oxford University Press 1997).

Warrich SA, '"Honour killings" and the law in Pakistan' in L Welchman and S Hossain (eds), *'Honour': Crimes, paradigms and violence against women* (Zed Books 2005).

Wasserstorm RA, 'Strict Liability in the Criminal Law' (1960) 12(4) Stanford Law Review 731.

Wasti T, 'Islamic Law in Practice: The Application of Qisas and Diyat Law in Pakistan' (2006) 13 Yearbook of Islamic and Middle Eastern Law 97.

Welchman L and Hossain S, 'Introduction: "Honour," rights and wrongs', in L Welchman and S Hossain (eds), *'Hon-*

our': Crimes, paradigms and violence against women (Zed Books 2005).

Yadav H, 'Honour Killings-An In-Depth study' (2012) Shamsher Bahadur Saxena College of Law <https://papers.ssrn.com/sol3/papers.cfm?abstract_id=2034965> accessed 26 July 2021.

Youssef N, 'Cultural Ideals, Feminine Behaviour and Family Control' (1973) 15 *Comparative Studies in Society and History* 326.

NGO Publications

Brohi N, *Women, Violence and Jirgas: Consensus and Impunity in Pakistan* (NCSW 2017).

Equality Now, 'Pakistan - The Qanun-e-Shahadat Order, 1984 (Law of Evidence)' <www.equalitynow.org/pakistan_the_qanun_e_shahadat_order_1984_law_of_evidence> accessed 26 July 2021.

Honour Based Violence Awareness Network, 'Honour Based Violence Awareness Network: Human Rights Country Report of 2018' <http://hbv-awareness.com/statistics-data/#Pakistan> accessed 26 July 2021.

Honour Based Violence Awareness Network, 'Honour Based Violence Awareness Network: Human Rights Country Report of 2018' <http://hbv-awareness.com/statistics-data/#India> accessed 26 July 2021.

Hughes L, 'India-Pakistan Relations – Part Three: Economic and Cultural Aspects' (2016) Future Directions International <www.futuredirections.org.au/wp-content/uploads/2016/10/India-Pakistan-Relations-%E2%80%93-Part-Three-Economic-and-Cultural-Aspects.pdf> accessed 26 July 2021.

Human Rights Watch, 'Integration of the Human Rights of Women and the Gender Perspective: Violence against Women and "Honour" Crimes (2001) Intervention at the 57th Session of the U.N. Commission on Human Rights.

Jaffrelot C, 'The Fate of Secularism in India' (2019) Carnegie Endowment for International Peace <https://carnegieendowment.org/2019/04/04/fate-of-secularism-in-india-pub-78689> accessed 26 July 2021.

Lari MZ, 'A Pilot Study on Honour Killings in Pakistan and Compliance of Law' [2011] Aurat Publication and Information Service Foundation <www.af.org.pk/pub_files/1366345831.pdf> accessed 26 July 2021.

National Human Rights Commission, India, 'Vision & Mission' <https://nhrc.nic.in/about-us/vision-and-mission> accessed 26 July 2121.

Omer R and Vardaan S, 'Authority without Accountability: The Search for Justice in Pakistan' (2013) International Commission of Jurors.

Parliamentarians for Global Action, 'Campaign for the Abolition of the Death Penalty' <www.pgaction.org/ilhr/adp/?gclid=EAIaIQobChMIwIivz4K78QIVGIjVCh2_yAYvEAAYASAAEgKNEfD_BwE> accessed 26 July 2021.

Vaishanav M 'Religious Nationalism and India's Future, Carnegie Endowment for International Peace<https://carnegieendowment.org/2019/04/04/religious-nationalism-and-india-s-future-pub-78703> accessed 26 July 2021.

Wright V, 'Deterrence in Criminal Justice, Evaluating Certainty vs. Severity of Punishment' [2010] The Sentencing Project.

Government Publications

Government of Pakistan, *Report of the Commission of Inquiry for Women* (1997, Government of Pakistan).

Human Rights Commission of Pakistan, 'HRCP Annual Report 2015' [2015] <http://hrcp-web.org/hrcpweb/hrcp-annual-report-2015/> accessed 26 July 2021.

National Commission for Human Rights, 'A Study on Honour Killings in Pakistan and Recommendatory Checks through Law' [2019] The Office of the Chairman, National Commission for Human Rights, Government of Pakistan <https://nchr.gov.pk/wp-content/uploads/2019/01/Final-Report-Honour-Killing.pdf> accessed 26 July 2021.

National Crime Records Bureau (NCRB), 'Crime in India – 2018' [2019] National Crime Report Bureau Ministry of Home Affairs <https://ncrb.gov.in/en/crime-india-2018#> accessed 26 July 2021.

Second Law Commission for India, Report, 13 December 1885.

US State Department, 'Pakistan 2019 Human Rights Report' (2019) <www.state.gov/wp-content/uploads/2020/03/PAKISTAN-2019-HUMAN-RIGHTS-REPORT.pdf> accessed 26 July 2021.

United Nations' Publications

Office of the High Commissioner for Human Rights (OHCHR), '15 Years of the United Nations Special Rapporteur on Violence against Women, Its Causes and Consequences' <www.ohchr.org/Documents/Issues/Women/15yearreviewofVAWMandate.pdf> accessed 26 July 2021.

UNGA, 'Report of the Committee on the Elimination of All Forms of Discrimination against Women General Recommendations'.

UN Global Compact, 'Endorse the Women's Empowerment Principles' https://www.unglobalcompact.org/take-action/action/womens-principles#:~:text=Take%20action%20across%20all%20-seven,all%20women%20and%20men%20workers. <https://www.unglobalcompact.org/take-action/action/womens-principles#:~:text=Take%20action%20across%20all%20-seven,all%20women%20and%20men%20workers> accessed 26 July 2021.

Websites

Aggarwal P, 'Social Alteration in the Institution of Marriage in India' (Academike, 2014) <www.lawctopus.com/academike/social-alteration-in-the-institution-of-marriage-in-india/#> accessed 26 July 2021.

Deshpande MS, 'History of the Indian Caste System and Its Impact on India Today' (California Polytechnic, 2010) <https://digitalcommons.calpoly.edu/socssp/44/> accessed 26 July 2021.

Javed R, 'Afzal Kohistani Murder: Family Ends Protest Following Protracted Negotiations with the Police' Dawn (Pakistan, 7 March 2019) <www.dawn.com/news/1468197> accessed 26 July 2021.

Verma A, 'Khap Panchayat: Informal Justice vs Formal Justice' (iPleaders, 2020) <https://blog.ipleaders.in/khap-Panchayat-informal-justice-vs-formal-justice/> accessed 26 July 2021.

Media Articles

'Alternate Dispute Resolution Bill Approved' *Dawn* (9 January 2017) <www.dawn.com/news/1309323> accessed 26 July 2021.

'Honour Killings: More than 300 Cases in the Last Three Years' *Times of India* (22 September 2018) <https://timesofindia.indiatimes.com/india/honour-killings-more-than-300-cases-in-last-three-years/articleshow/65908947.cms> accessed 26 July 2021.

Ali I, '510 Women, 259 Men Fell Prey to "Honour" Killings during Five Years in Sindh' *Dawn* (19 February 2020) <www.dawn.com/news/1535295> accessed 26 July 2021.

Ali U, 'Cover Story: Murder in the Name of Honour' *Newsline* (August 2016) <https://newslinemagazine.com/magazine/murder-name-honour/> accessed 26 July 2021.

Ali YA, 'Understanding Pashtunwali' *The Nation* (6 August 2013) <https://nation.com.pk/06-Aug-2013/understanding-pashtunwali> accessed 26 July 2021.

Ananthakrishnan G, 'Improve Representation of Women in the Judiciary, Sensitize Judges: AG to SC' *The Indian Express* (3 December 2020) <https://indianexpress.com/article/india/improve-representation-of-women-in-judiciary-sensitise-judges-ag-to-sc-7079925/> accessed 26 July 2021.

Ansari N, 'Biased/Unbiased: The Parallel Justice System in Rural Pakistan - A Close Scrutiny' *The Express Tribune* (Karachi, 26 February 2014) <https://tribune.com.pk/story/676185/biasedunbiased-the-parallel-justice-system-in-rural-pakistan-a-close-scrutiny> 26 July 2021.

Baloch SM, 'Pakistan Authorities Records a Dozen Cases of Honour Killing in a Fortnight' *The Guardian* (17 May 2019) <www.theguardian.com/global-development/2019/

may/17/pakistan-authorities-record-a-dozen-cases-of-honour-killing-in-a-fortnight> accessed 26 July 2021.

Chaudhary, DR, Feudal mindset: In hearts of darkness. *Deccan Herald* (1 August 2010).

Dhingra S, 'Revenge Rape, Honour Killings as "Justice": Pakistan's Problematic Jirgas Get More Power' (*The Print*, 2017) <https://theprint.in/report/revenge-rape-honour-killings-justice-pakistan-jirgas/13878/>accessed 26 July 2021.

Doris J, 'A Conversation with Margaret Visser: Diagnosing That Feeling of Helplessness' *Catholic New Times* (Toronto, 1 May 2003).

Farmer B, 'Mukhtar Mai, Pakistan's Gang Rape Survivor, Vows She Will Not Back Down as She Fights on for Justice' *The Telegraph* (Islamabad, 10 March 2019) <www.telegraph.co.uk/global-health/women-and-girls/mukhtar-mai-pakistans-gang-rape-survivor-sets-school-fights/> accessed 26 July 2021.

Gannon K, 'A Woman Sacrificed for Honor of Her Family' *LA Times* (Lahore, 9 July 2000) <www.latimes.com/archives/la-xpm-2000-jul-09-mn-50070-story.html> 26 July 2021.

Hashim A, 'How a Pakistani Whistle-Blower was Killed for "Honour"' (*Al Jazeera*, 2019) <www.aljazeera.com/features/2019/3/26/how-a-pakistani-whistle-blower-was-killed-for-honour> accessed 26 July 2021.

Imranullah SM, 'Madras High Court Sets Aside Death Sentence Awarded to Prime Accused in 2016 Udumalpet Shankar Murder Case' The Hindu (Chennai, 22 June 2020) <www.thehindu.com/news/national/tamil-nadu/madras-high-court-sets-aside-death-awarded-to-prime-accused-in-2016-udumalpet-shankar-murder-case/article31887684.ece>accessed 26 July 2021.

Janardhanan A, 'Udumalpet Honour Killing: Shankar's Father-in-Law Acquitted by Madras HC' *The Indian Express* (Chennai, 22 June 2020) <https://indianexpress.com/article/cities/chennai/udumalpet-honour-killing-shankars-father-in-law-acquitted-by-madras-hc-6470569/> accessed 26 July 2021.

Khan MH, 'Editorial' *Women's Weekly* (June 1967).

Krishnan K, '"Honor" Crimes in India: An Assault on Women's Autonomy' *Al Jazeera* (2018) <www.aljazeera.-com/opinions/2018/3/14/honour-crimes-in-india-an-assault-on-womens-autonomy> accessed 26 July 2021.

Krishnan K, 'Nirupama's Murder: The Violence of the High-Born' *Counter Currents* (26 May 2010) <www.countercur-rents.org/krishnan260510.htm> accessed 26 July 2021.

Maher S, 'Viewpoint: Qandeel Balouch was Killed for Making Lives Difficult' *BBC* (30 September 2019) <www.bbc.com/news/world-asia-49874994> accessed 26 July 2021.

Naqvi F, 'The Curious Case of the Shariat Court' *The News* (10 January 2016) <www.thenews.com.pk/print/89285-The-curious-case-of-the-Shariat-Court> accessed 26 July 2021.

Omer R, 'Gender Imbalance in Law' *Dawn* (15 March 2016) <www.dawn.com/news/1245694> accessed 26 July 2021.

Pal S, 'Conviction Rates Remain Low, While Encounter "Jus-tice" Increases' *NewsClick* (2019) <www.newsclick.in/con-viction-rates-remain-low-while-encounter-justice-increas-es> accessed 26 July 2021.

PTI. (2014). Retrieved from https://www.ptinews.com

Ram N, 'Visakhapatnam: Honor Killings on the Rise' *Deccan Chronicle* (Vishakapatnam, 18 September 2018) <www.deccanchronicle.com/nation/crime/180918/visakha-patnam-honour-killings-on-the-rise.html> accessed 26 July 2021.

Rukmini S, 'The Many Shades of Rape Cases in Delhi' *The Hindu* (New Delhi, 29 July 2014) <www.thehindu.com/data/the-many-shades-of-rape-cases-in-delhi/article6261042.ece> accessed 26 July 2021.

Sarkar G, 'Death sentence for daughter murder, Bhagalpur' *Times of India* (30 January 2015) www.timesofindis.indiatime.com/2015/1/30/archivelist/ year/2015.

Shah UM, 'Caste-Driven Honor Killings Still Haunt India' *UCA News* (23 May 2019) <www.ucanews.com/news/caste-driven-honor-killings-still-haunt-india/85209#> accessed 26 July 2021.

The Asian Age. (2003). Retrieved from www.asianage.com

The Times of India. (2002). Retrieved from www.timesofindia.com UNFPA. (2004). Retrieved from https://www.unfpa.org

Reports, Studies & Comments

Amnesty International, *Pakistan: Women's Human Rights Remain a Dead Letter: No Progress Towards the Realization of Women's Rights After the Ratification of the Convention on the Elimination of All Forms of Discrimination Against Women* (March 1997, AI Index: ASA 33/07/97, *Amnesty International*). <link> accessed 26 July 2021.

Amnesty International, *Pakistan: No Progress on Women's Rights* (September 1998, AI Index: ASA 33/13/98, *Amnesty International*). <link> accessed 26 July 2021.

Amnesty International, *Pakistan: Violence against Women in the Name of Honour* (September 1999, AI Index: ASA 33/17/99, *Amnesty International*). <link> accessed 26 July 2021.

Amnesty International, *Pakistan: Honour Killings of Girls and Women* (1999, ASA 33/18/99, *Amnesty International)* <http://www.amnesty.org/en/library/asset/ASA33/018/1999/en/9fe83c27-e0f1-11dd-be39-2d4003be4450/asa330181999en.pdf> accessed 26 July 2021.

Amnesty International, *Broken Bodies, Shattered Minds Torture, and Ill-Treatment of Women* (2001, *Amnesty International*). http://www.amnesty.org/en/library/info/ACT40/001/2001 accessed 26 July 2021.

Amnesty International, *Pakistan: Insufficient Protection of Women* (2002, Al Index: ASA/33/006/2002, *Amnesty International*) http://www.amnesty.org/en/library/asset/ASA33/006/2002/en/b734002a-d873-11dd-9df8-936c90684588/asa330062002en.pdf accessed 26 July 2021.

Amnesty International, *Pakistan: The Tribal Justice System* (2002, Al Index: ASA/33/024/2002, *Amnesty International*) http://www.amnesty.org/en/library/asset/ASA33/024/2002/en/293987eb-d812-11dd-9df8- 936c90684588/asa330242002en.pdf accessed 26 July 2021.

Dimri S, 'Social Interventions into Anti-Social Actions: Critical Legal Analysis of Honour Killings' (2019, *Bharati Law Review*) <https://papers.ssrn.com/sol3/papers.cfm?abstract_id=3759280> accessed 26 July 2021.

Godara AK, 'Honour Killing and Role of Khap Panchayat: An Empirical Study' (2012) <http://14.139.58.147:8080/jspui/bitstream/123456789/47/1/07LLM12.pdf> accessed 26 July 2021.

Human Rights Watch, *Crime or Custom? Violence against Women in Pakistan* (1999, Human Rights Watch).

Knudsen A, 'License to Kill: Honour Killings in Pakistan' (2004, *CMI Reports*) http://www.cmi.no/pdf/?

file=/publications/2004/wp/wp2004-1.pdf accessed 26 July 2021.

LeBlanc PD, 'Indus Epigraphic Perspectives: Exploring Past Decipherment Attempts & Possible New Approaches' (Master's thesis, University of Ottawa 2013).

Nelson MJ, 'Islamic Law in an Islamic Republic: What Role for Parliament?' (School of Oriental and African Studies, 2015) <https://eprints.soas.ac.uk/22295/1/Nelson_Islamic%20Law%20in%20an%20Islamic%20Republic.pdf> accessed 26 July 2021.

Rashid SA, 'Jirga System and Women's Rights' (*Pakistan Today,* 2021) <www.pakistantoday.com.pk/2021/03/12/Jirga-system-and-womens-rights/> accessed 26 July 2021.

Razvi M, *A Study of Formal and Parallel Legal Systems Prevalent in Pakistan* (*National Commission on Status of Women*, 2011) <www.ncsw.gov.pk/SiteImage/Downloads/A%20Study%20of%20Formal%20and%20Parallel%20Legal%20Systems%20Prevalent%20in%20Pakistan.pdf> accessed 26 July 2021.

Shah HQ, *There is no 'Honour' in Killing. Don't Let them Get Away with Murder (Booklet on Criminal Procedures)* (Shirkat Gah, 2002).

Shahid U, 'Inquest into Justice of the Pakistani Customary "Panchayat Justice System" in the context of the International Human Rights Law' (Master's thesis, University of London 2012) <https://core.ac.uk/download/pdf/13120138.pdf?repositoryId=99> accessed 26 July 2021.

Shirkat Gah/Women Living Under Muslim Laws, *Chart of Customary Practices in Pakistan in Comparison with Statutory Law: Women & Law Pakistan Country Project* (SP Creative Design, 1995).

About the Author

Mohammed Subhan Hussain is a doctoral researcher in Law at the Institute of Advanced Legal Studies (IALS), University of London, specialising in commercial fraud litigation. He also specialises in South Asian Laws (India and Pakistan), encompassing five main areas of research: Violence Against Women (VAW); Honour Killings; Nuptial Concerns; Divorce; and Reproductive Rights.

If you enjoyed this book, please consider leaving an online review. The author would appreciate reading your thoughts.

About the Publisher

Sulis International Press publishes select fiction and nonfiction in a variety of genres under four imprints: Riversong Books, Sulis Academic Press, Sulis Press, and Keledei Publications.

For more, visit the website at
https://sulisinternational.com

Subscribe to the newsletter at
https://sulisinternational.com/subscribe/

Follow on social media
https://www.facebook.com/SulisInternational
https://twitter.com/Sulis_Intl
https://www.pinterest.com/Sulis_Intl/
https://www.instagram.com/sulis_international/

Made in the USA
Monee, IL
05 November 2026

67845323R00132